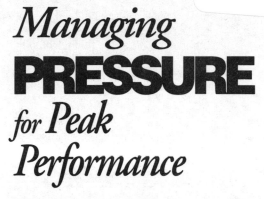

Managing
PRESSURE
for Peak
Performance

Managing
PRESSURE
for Peak Performance

**THE
POSITIVE
APPROACH
TO STRESS**

*Stephen
Williams*

**KOGAN
PAGE**

To my father and all the people who have given me the opportunity to learn from them. Thank you for your support encouragement and wisdom.

First published in 1994

Kogan Page Limited
120 Pentonville Road
London N1 9JN
© Stephen Williams, 1994

British Library Cataloguing in Publication Data

A CIP record for this book is available from the British Library.

ISBN 0 7494 1239 9 (Paperback) 0 7494 1409 X (Hardback)

Typeset by BookEns Limited, Baldock, Herts SG7 6NW
Printed in England by Clays Ltd, St. Ives plc

Contents

Part 2 Action

Introduction

This book is about the relationship between pressure, stress and peak performance. The central theme is that stress is not inevitable; it is just one possible outcome of being under pressure. We can control the way we respond to pressure so that we produce positive results rather than negative stress. Pressure can be used to stimulate peak performance.

The book is in two parts. Part 1 is about understanding the issues.

• What happens when we are under pressure?

• What is stress?

• What is peak performance?

Stress is a confusing and imprecise term, and Part I explains exactly what happens when we suffer from stress. It analyses the stress process, explains the difference between stress and pressure, and shows the relationship between pressure and performance. The key to managing pressure is to understand the process, and recognise where, when and how to intervene.

Part 2 is about taking action. It describes a variety of techniques for managing pressure, and shows how taking control and making positive choices can turn pressure into peak performance. This section of the book includes practical 'stress tips' to help manage pressure and covers topics such as:

• positive choices;

• positive thinking;

- self-limiting beliefs;
- relaxation;
- time management;
- home and work ;
- communication skills;
- emotional detachment;
- being yourself.

This book is based on my experiences of helping individuals and their organisations to improve their ability to manage pressure. It has been written to show how pressure can be used to enhance performance instead of producing stress. It is not prescriptive, but describes what works and what is successful.

Many of the techniques will be familiar to you and most of them are common sense. The problem with common sense is that it gets overruled by common practice. We know what we should do but we don't do it because we have developed bad habits. We need to break our established patterns and actively manage pressure. We need to be in control. I hope the book will help you to review the way you manage pressure and encourage you to make a difference.

Control starts with understanding the issues and making choices. You are the only person who really knows how you respond to pressure. Choose what works for you and enjoy your success.

Part 1
Understanding

I suppose it started with Simon. Simon was a hardware development manager, young, hard working and well regarded. He'd been with the company for 4 or 5 years, had had 3 promotions and was now running a team of 50 people. Simon came into my office looking worried, sat down and started to talk.

'I don't know what it is. I'm not sleeping well, I don't seem to get as much done as I used to and I'm missing the deadlines on my projects. I've been getting in early, working late and taking my work home but I still can't get on top of things. I hardly ever see my wife and kids, and when I do I seem to spend all my time falling out with them. It's really getting me down. When I come into work in the morning I start getting pains in my stomach and, by the time I drive into the car park, my stomach feels as if there is a tight knot twisting inside it. This has been going on for weeks now and it seems to be getting worse. I've also started to get aches in my neck and shoulders, but I think that's probably to do with driving to work. I don't think I'm ill, but there's definitely something wrong. What do you think I should do?'

We talked for an hour about Simon's workload, the missed deadlines and his problems at home. Simon agreed to see his doctor when he had time. We never mentioned stress. In 1978 no one talked about stress at work. Five days later, Simon had an accident on the way to work. He was unhurt but the other driver died. Simon can't remember what happened but he thinks he may have lost concentration for a moment. I still wonder if I could have done more.

Stress is insidious. It creeps up on us slowly and changes our lives. Most of us are not aware of being under stress until something happens which makes us realise just how bad we feel and, by then, it's too late. By the time we recognise the problem, our health, our job, our family and our relationships may all have suffered. In managing stress, as in all illness, prevention is better than cure. The worst time to deal with stress is when we are suffering from it. By that stage our resources are diminished. We are not thinking clearly and we may be in such a negative frame of mind that failing to manage stress becomes a self-fulfilling prophecy.

Simon had been a successful manager. He had worked under enormous pressure for years and, for most of that time, had produced excellent results. He had been promoted after only six months with the firm and, since then, had taken every project in his stride. Simon was the sort of person who seemed to thrive on pressure, he worked hard, he worked his team hard and he got results. Simon, like many of the other young managers in the company, was a success. He kept hitting his targets and was rewarded by more responsibility, bigger projects and tighter deadlines. His company, like many organisations, kept raising the height of the bar. Every jump had to be higher than the one before. Then one day it happened; Simon failed to clear the bar. He missed the deadline. Simon wasn't the only one to fail, but he was one of the few who talked about their problems. All around the company people were in trouble; good employees resigned, sickness absence increased, productivity dropped and quality declined. Success turned to failure and people suffered. What went wrong? Why did a group of enthusiastic, intelligent, capable people cease to thrive on pressure and start to suffer from stress? What could have been done to prevent the decline?

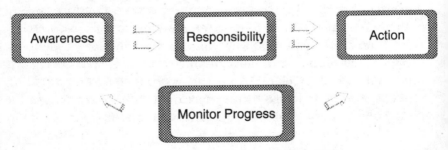

Figure 1 : Awareness Responsibility Action

THE BUILDING BLOCKS OF CHANGE

The successful management of pressure is based on a simple model that shows the need for awareness, responsibility and action in initiating and managing change.

Raise awareness

Managing pressure starts with awareness. It's hard to manage without understanding; we can't deal with something unless we know it's there. The problem with managing stress is that we get so wrapped up in our problems we stop thinking clearly. People under pressure are often the last to know that they have a problem. They are so preoccupied with dealing with the issues, meeting the deadline or hitting the target that they lose the ability to see what is happening to them. It is only when other people start to talk or the pressure eases off that they recognise they have been suffering from stress. Sometimes recognition comes too late. The pressure has gone on for too long and stress has taken its toll. Mental and physical health is impaired, and relationships with family, friends and colleagues are damaged. We need to improve our ability to recognise the warning signs in order to take prompt remedial action.

Some people find that raising their awareness of the stress process directly improves their ability to manage pressure. They anticipate problems and take evasive action. They prevent pressure from leading to stress and circumvent the need for further action.

Accept responsibility

You are responsible for managing your pressure. Other people may help but they cannot do it for you. A common response to pressure is to blame someone else for causing the problem: 'My boss dumped this on me at the last minute, how can I possibly get it done on time?' People also blame their circumstances for avoiding taking action: 'If it weren't for ...' is a frequently heard excuse for not acting. 'If only ...' is the other side of the same coin. Wishing that things hadn't happened the way they did or wishing that things will happen in a certain way in the future are both barriers to achieving change. As long as we hang on to a belief that other people or our circumstances need to change before we change we will be powerless. Action starts within us. We are the instigators of change. We need to take personal responsibility for our future and work with what we've got. Managing pressure is about 'being here now'. Deal with the present and manage the future. We will never manage pressure as long as we think that it's someone else's responsibility to do it for us. It is our life, our pressure and our responsibility, and we should seize the opportunity to manage it ourselves.

Take action

The third and most important element in the process of managing pressure is to take action. The universe rewards action, not thought. There are millions of people who think up wonderful ways for making money. Only the ones who do something about it get rich. Unless we do something with our knowledge we may as well remain ignorant. Awareness and responsibility achieve nothing without action. It is like walking across a road and seeing a bus coming towards you. You can be aware that the bus is getting closer and recognise that, unless you do something, it's likely to hit you. You may also decide it's your responsibility to jump out of the way. However, unless you move, unless you take action, awareness and responsibility are a waste of time. You end up as dead as someone who failed to see the bus in the first place.

Monitor progress

The final element in managing pressure is to monitor progress. To manage pressure actively we need to know that our actions are having the desired effect. We need feedback to ensure that we build on our strengths and compensate for our weaknesses. Stress reduces our ability to recognise changes in our behaviour, and we often fail to appreciate the effect that stress has on our work, our physical and mental health, and our relations with other people. Unless we monitor consciously our ability to manage pressure, we run the risk of slipping into a pattern of behaviour that produces stress instead of high performance. Monitoring progress simply makes this stage explicit and reminds us of the need to be sensitive to change.

1

Stress, Pressure and Performance

Geoff and Graham are teachers. They work at the same school and teach the same subject. Geoff is a few years older than Graham but, apart from that, they're very similar. They're good friends outside school and their families spend a lot of time with each other. Geoff loves his job. He likes the kids, he enjoys the work and tries to make his lessons as interesting as possible.

Graham doesn't understand how Geoff gets so much done. He finds every day a struggle. The kids are difficult, the lessons never seem to go quite as he planned and he can't get on top of the marking. Graham rushes everywhere. He's never quite on time for the lessons and always seems to be running down corridors, clutching a pile of books. He knows he's disorganised but thinks there aren't enough hours in the day to do everything he has to do. He has trouble in the evenings because school work takes up far too much time and it conflicts with his home life. Quite often, Geoff suggests they go out for a drink but Graham can't make it because he has too much work to do.

The school is about to appoint a new head of department and both Graham and Geoff have applied for the job. Who will get it?

Graham and Geoff do identical jobs. They teach the same subject in the same school to similar kids. Their home and family circumstances are also very similar. The sources of pressure are the same for both Graham and Geoff, yet Geoff thrives on pressure while Graham falls apart. For Geoff, the pressure produces peak performance, for Graham it produces stress. Why?

THE DIFFERENCE BETWEEN PRESSURE AND STRESS

Managing pressure starts with understanding the difference between pressure and stress. Stress is different from pressure but the two terms are often used as synonyms. This creates confusion and adds to the difficulty in understanding what happens when we are under pressure.

Stress

Stress has been described as one of the most inaccurate words in scientific literature. The basic problem is that the word stress is used to describe both the sources and the effects of the stress process. We say we are under stress when we are in a difficult situation or are put under pressure. Stress, in this context, refers to a stimulus or an input. We also say we are under stress when we are suffering from anxiety or depression, or simply can't cope. In this case stress is a response or an outcome.

The failure to reach a consensus on the definition of the term adds to the general confusion about the nature of stress and allows senior managers to deny they have a problem with stress at work. The fact that stress has many definitions does not mean it doesn't exist. In that respect, stress is a little like love. Love may mean different things to different people and it may be hard to get people to agree on a common definition. However, we know what it feels like to experience the emotion, and the feeling of being 'in love' or 'under stress' does not become less real because we find it difficult to describe.

Throughout this book we will make a clear distinction between pressure and stress. Pressure is the input or the start of the process. Stress is an outcome or a possible response to pressure. The process by which pressure becomes stress is called the stress process and is explained in more detail in Chapter 2.

Stress is what happens to us when things go wrong. It is something we suffer from and has a negative quality. It has a physical, a psychological and an emotional component. There does not need to be any external cause, and the consequences of being under stress can affect our physical, mental and social health. The effects of stress are far-reaching and have an impact on every aspect of our lives. However, stress is not inevitable. It is an outcome of a complex, interactive process and, as we will see later in the book, we can intervene at various stages of that process to avoid the stress outcome. The bad news is that stress is so widespread it has been described as the twentieth-century plague. The good news is that, unlike the plague, we can decide whether or not we get it.

Differentiating between pressure and stress makes it clear that stress is bad for us and pressure is the force that may produce stress. When managers understand the difference between stress and pressure they cannot argue that their staff need more stress. The managers may want more pressure, and they usually want higher performance, but they do not want more stress.

Pressure

Pressure is inevitable. We cannot go through life without experiencing pressure and attempting to avoid pressure is running away. Pressure needs to be managed and, what is more important, it needs to be actively managed. It is not a passive process and it's not one that lends itself to a 'one shot' solution. There are no silver bullets for dealing with pressure. We have to work at the management of pressure and work at it throughout our lives. Pressure stops when you stop. 'Life's a bitch and then you die'.

Pressure is a neutral force. It can produce either good or bad outcomes, depending on an individual's adaptability and coping skills. Pressure can be the stimulus we need to enjoy our lives, learn new skills, experience excitement and get things done. It can also be the force that causes depression and anxiety, makes us fail to complete projects, miss deadlines, break up relationships and become seriously ill. In other words pressure can either help to raise performance or cause stress. The same pressure can produce either of these responses and the way we react to pressure, combined with our adaptability, governs the outcome of the stress process. The following diagram shows this process in more detail.

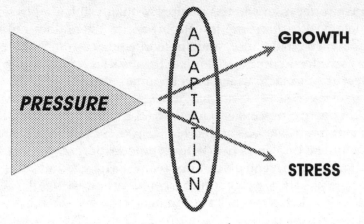

Figure 2: The outcome of pressure.

We need pressure to grow. If we try to avoid stress by eliminating pressure we will atrophy or produce new pressures. Imagine a busy executive who decides that he can't take it any more and is going to drop out of the rat race to grow vegetables or live on a beach in Spain. The executive can escape from the pressures of his executive life. He no longer has to worry about commuting, going to meetings or playing office politics. At first the change may be successful, for there is a honeymoon period where the old pressures are no longer there and everything seems positive. However, before too long, new pressures start making themselves known, such as the pressure of finding enough money to live on, the pressure of physical labour or, strange as it may seem, the pressure of too much leisure. Boredom and burnout both kill.

Eliminating pressure is not the solution to avoiding stress. We need to manage pressure, not to remove it. Managing pressure means managing our response to pressure and our perception of pressure. We must work with what we've got.

Performance

Pressure produces peak performance. We work at our best when we are stimulated and stretched, not when we are bored and constrained. The link between pressure and performance can be traced back to the dawn of human evolution when men and women developed a set of responses to improve their chances of survival when faced with a physical threat. Life depended on the ability to react to danger with speed and strength, and our bodies found a way of producing that little bit extra to make the difference between life and death. Pressure became a trigger for enhanced performance because our normal state of functioning does not provide the energy or resources we need to deal with a physical threat at our optimum level. The mechanism for producing enhanced performance is known as the flight or fight response. We perceive a threat and our nervous system triggers complex changes in our body chemistry to channel our resources into a sudden surge of energy, and a switch into peak performance. The physical changes in our body as a result of this reaction are responsible for stress-related illness and are described in detail in Chapter 2.

These automatic responses are still useful today. They come into play in moments of crisis when we need to make an extraordinary effort to deal with danger. It is these chemical and hormonal changes in our bodies that allow someone to lift a car to free a friend trapped underneath or walk for miles with an injured leg to get help. The stress response is also useful in sports and competitive games when it provides that little bit of extra performance needed to achieve success. The flight or fight response is also useful in a work environment when we need additional resources to accomplish a task.

The flight or fight response is there because it helps us to survive. It's an essential part of our physiology and we cannot turn it off. Under the appropriate circumstances our reaction to stress can save our lives. Unfortunately these physical changes can also be extremely damaging. The flight or fight response is a defence mechanism that has evolved to produce a physical response to a physical threat. It is also a short term response to a short term threat. Today the threats tend to be mental rather than physical and they last a lot longer. These changes make our inbuilt defence mechanisms redundant. A physical response is inappropriate. A rapid burst of energy doesn't get us out of trouble. It is as if we have spent years training and developing our bodies to be the world's best boxer only to find, as we enter the ring, that the rules have been changed and we're playing chess. The stress response is therefore, on most occasions, a redundant response. It is also a damaging response because we have no way of turning the

Figure 3: *The flight or fight response.*

released energy into physical energy. If the threat continues, our bodies continue to release more chemicals and hormones. Eventually the effects of exposure to a continued threat will become harmful and produce stress.

THE PRESSURE–PERFORMANCE CURVE

The relationship between pressure and performance varies from person to person, and from time to time. Sometimes moderate pressure will produce good performance; at other times it will result in stress. However, it is possible to illustrate the relationship between these two variables by plotting typical responses on a graph.

The graph shows five separate stages; boredom, comfort, stretch, strain and panic. The boundary between these stages is blurred and the pressure required to produce a given level of performance will vary from person to person. The graph shows that people can have a problem at both ends of the pressure scale. Too little pressure or too much pressure can both be harmful. At one end of the scale we have a pressure overload. People can no longer cope and may suffer from a major mental or physical breakdown. This is known as 'burnout'. At the other extreme people have so little stimulation they become lethargic and lose their ability to cope with everyday life. This lack of pressure or stimulation over long periods of time is called 'rustout'.

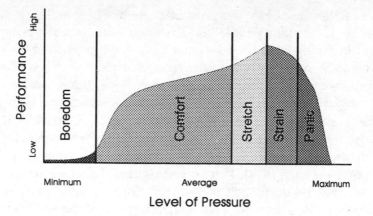

Figure 1: Pressure-performance stages.

Low pressure

Imagine a job without pressure. You arrive at work in the morning and know exactly what you will be doing. The role never changes, there is no stimulation and no challenge. Peter, a factory operative in a soft drink bottling factory, has a low pressure job:

> My job is to mix the concentrate with water before the drinks are bottled. I get to work at eight and press one button to turn on my machine. It's a big vat in a room by itself so there is no one else around me. The machine starts to fill the vat with concentrate and water, and I have to watch it so I can stop it when it gets full. It takes 20 minutes to fill and mix so I just sit there for all this time. There's no real pressure because there's an alarm that goes off if I forget to stop the machine at the right level. I then go for lunch and do the same thing in the afternoon. Then its time to go home. Basically my job is to press one start and one stop button 20 times a day.

Peter is bored by his job. He appears to have no pressure but is suffering from stress. His day is a slow torture of mindless, frustrating inactivity. Peter lacks stimulation. He needs a challenge or some variety to make his day interesting and give him something

23

to do. Peter may be an extreme example but he is not an isolated case. We meet many people in many organisations with boring and stress-inducing jobs. They may not have enough to do or the work may not be sufficiently stimulating. Researchers into the relationship between stress and work demands have found that workers involved in jobs with high workload and low discretion have poor mental health and higher risk of heart disease.[1] A job that consists of a high volume of repetitive, undemanding tasks is probably one of the most stressful. However, the pressure performance curve is different for each of us. Peter's colleague, John, does an identical job and has no desire to change. He enjoys the time to think and daydream. He also has a very demanding social life and finds that he can compensate for the inactivity of the day with his evenings out, his family and his role as secretary of the local gardening club. The pressure on John is within his comfort zone.

The comfort zone

The comfort zone, as its name suggests, is where we feel most comfortable. We have some stimulation and some challenge, but we are not really pushed. This is the area where most of us spend most of our lives. There is nothing wrong with being comfortable. It gives us the opportunity to maintain a balance in our lives and allows us to achieve reasonable results. We may feel under some pressure from time to time but it's nothing to worry about and we quickly revert to normal. Sometimes we can be too comfortable and become complacent. Work settles into a steady routine. We get set in our ways and find it hard to respond to change. We need the occasional challenge to keep us alert and motivated. From time to time we need to be stretched.

The stretch zone

As pressure increases beyond our comfort level we get into the stretch zone. This is where we know we're under pressure and feel stimulated. We face challenges and new experiences, learn from these experiences and, as a result, go through a period of growth and development. Our confidence and self-esteem increase as we continue to meet new challenges. We develop our resources, improve our skills and become better equipped to face even greater challenges in the future. The stretch zone is the area of peak performance. We feel stimulated, energised and confident, and function in a resourceful, successful state.

Strain

Problems arise when pressure continues to increase, we start to find we can no longer continue to manage and we become 'over-stretched'. At this point our coping mechanisms start to break down and performance deteriorates. The same problem occurs when we have been working under pressure for long periods of time and have exhausted our ability to cope. The strain has become too great and growth has turned into stress. Strain can be managed if we are alert to the warning signs and can take remedial action. Sometimes seeing the light at the end of the tunnel is enough: 'If I can just get this report finished I'll be able to relax'.

Panic

Panic is when the world collapses around us and we are unable to take any more. This sudden and dramatic failure can be very damaging, both for the individual and the organisation. It is as if something has snapped inside us and everything we do is wrong. If we try to continue to operate in the panic zone we run the risk of serious illness. At this stage our suffering is obvious to others. We may not be aware of our problems, but our family and our colleagues know something is wrong. In this area stress becomes pathological and people may need professional help or have to make significant changes in their lives before they return to normal functioning. The panic zone is dangerous, so avoid it if you can.

MANAGING THE PRESSURE–PERFORMANCE CURVE

Managing pressure for peak performance means managing the pressure–performance curve. You need to become sensitive to how pressure affects you and should try to manage your life so that you are in control of your pressure zone. Don't make the mistake of thinking that the absence of pressure is good, and that you should try and remove all pressure from your life. At the other extreme don't think that being under stress is tough and macho, and the more pressure you're under, the more you'll produce. Some people think that they can continue to take an excess of pressure for ever. They are sure that 'it's better to burn out than it is to rust'.

Unfortunately they are deceiving themselves, since no one is completely stress resistant and eventually something will give. We want to avoid both 'rustout' and 'burnout', and keep to optimum performance with the ability to switch on extraordinary performance when we need to meet exceptional demands.

Peak performance

Peak performance is a relative rather than an absolute concept. It isn't about being better than anyone else, although that may occur as a by-product of being in a peak state. Performance fluctuates from day to day and from hour to hour. We have good times and bad times, and we have good days and bad days. In striving for peak performance, we are trying to raise our own standards of personal excellence and achievement. To take a sporting analogy: it's not playing tennis to world championship level or beating the best in the country; it is being better today than you were yesterday and better tomorrow than you are today. It is continually improving your game against your standards.

Try to think back to a time when you produced excellent performance. A time, either at work or in your home life, when to coin a phrase 'you were on a roll' and simply couldn't do anything wrong. At that time you achieved what you set out to achieve, accomplished tasks and were totally successful in everything you tried to do. Peak performance is about living in that state. It is responding to the world as a capable, resourceful and enthusiastic person who thrives on challenge, and looks for opportunities to grow.

We can use the stimulus we get from being under pressure to enhance performance. It's a bit like sailing. One way of dealing with a strong wind is to take down the sails, batten down the hatches and ride out the storm. Another approach is to take a good position, rig the boat to suit the conditions and use the energy of the wind to speed the boat forward. Shutting down the systems and waiting for the storm to pass may avoid damage, but the boat doesn't go anywhere. Judging the conditions, making the appropriate adjustments and using the energy of the wind enables the boat to make progress. The skill is in judging when it's safe to run with the wind and when it's best to stay put.

Managing pressure for peak performance is about knowing when and how to use pressure to get things done. It's about the thrill of working to tight deadlines, doing things we didn't think we could do, meeting the challenge and producing a successful outcome. It is also, as with the sailing analogy, about knowing when the pressure is too great and holding on until the time is right for action. You choose when and how to act. You manage pressure; pressure doesn't manage you.

The pressure threshold

Everyone has a different pressure threshold. Some people can handle a lot of pressure while others fall apart very easily. The problem of managing other people's pressure is made more complex by the fact that the same person can cope with different levels of pressure at different times in their life. There are times when people are particularly vulnerable and a normally robust person will find themselves under stress. Pressure is cumulative. If someone is going through a difficult period at home, has financial worries, is just getting over the death of a close relative or their children are having problems at school, then their ability to take pressure at work will be greatly reduced. We need to be sensitive to the individual circumstances of the people who work for us and understand that there are times when we may need to reduce the demands we place upon them.

A person, like a pressure cooker, has a limited capacity. We can hold only so much before things overflow or explode. In Figure 5

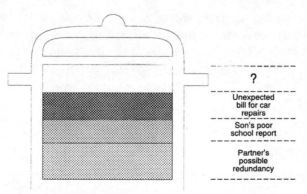

Figure 5: How much pressure can you take?

Event	✓
Moving house	
Death of partner, close friend or relative	
Marital problems	
Pregnancy	
Financial difficulty	
Legal problem	
Losing your job	
Difficult relationship with children	
Difficult relationship with parents	
Serious illness of yourself or close family member	

Figure 6: Life events.

we can see that worry about a partner's possible redundancy fills a third of the container. A quarter is filled by concern about a poor school report; another quarter is taken up with an unexpected bill. There isn't much room for left for other problems. Major life events can take us to the limit of our ability to manage pressure very quickly. The above table shows some of these events.

To be sensitive to the pressure we put other people under and be aware when we are pushing them too hard or giving them too little stimulation is incredibly difficult. It is as if you were walking a tightrope that's swinging from side to side and it changes every day for every person who works for you. If you have people working for you, think about the relationship between pressure and performance, and try to find the optimum level for yourself and each of your staff. It will be worth it.

Remember:

* different people have different pressure thresholds;

* the same person has different thresholds at different times;

* pressure is cumulative.

References

1   Karasek, R and Theorell, T (1990) *Healthy Work: Stress, Productivity, and the Reconstruction of Working Life:* Basic Books, New York.

2

Understanding the Stress Process

Other people noticed first. They saw the change in behaviour as John became increasingly distant and withdrawn. They wondered why he stopped saying hello when he came into work and why he'd lost his sense of humour. Sally, John's secretary, couldn't understand why he was so indecisive and she got upset when he started shouting at her for no apparent reason. Other people noticed that John was putting on weight, and looked pale and tired. He had an almost constant cold and had recently started having time off through illness. He didn't seem to have much energy and became more short tempered every day. People started to avoid him and his staff were terrified of having to tell him anything that might be seen as bad news. He would fly off the handle at the slightest provocation and had already lost one client as a result of a major mistake on an order.

His boss was worried about John's health and performance but he couldn't get John to discuss the subject. It appeared that John had problems at home but no one knew if that was the reason for his difficulties at work or if problems at work were causing problems at home. As the months went by John continued to get worse. His rudeness and unpleasantness became something of a joke and the people in his department were relieved that he was having so much time off sick.

John was devastated when they made him redundant. He knew he hadn't been well and had made a few mistakes recently but he never expected to lose his job. He had been with the company for over 20 years, had always been a good manager and thought he was regarded as a steady, reliable member of the management team. It was true that he had resisted the reorganisation that changed the role of his department and hadn't succeeded in making the productivity improvements the company expected, but he thought things were starting to settle down. Now he had lost everything. He had no job and his home life was a mess. He remembered he had been happy once; before the reorganisation and the pressure.

How do we recognise stress? The changes in John's behaviour and physical health are clear signs of stress, but John, his family and his colleagues failed to recognise that he was no longer coping with pressure. In John's case the stress process was one of gradual deterioration. He didn't have a sudden nervous breakdown or a heart attack. He found himself locked into a slow, downward spiral and, by the time he realised he had a problem, it was too late. It may have been possible to take remedial action if John had been more aware of the cause of his symptoms or his family and colleagues had been quicker to recognise the signs of stress. In retrospect it is obvious that John saw the reorganisation as a threat and was unable to adapt to the pressure. His failure to cope resulted in stress-related illness, but, because no one knew he had a problem, the real illness, the cause of the problem, went untreated. It is much easier to treat the symptoms than the real, underlying issues, particularly if the cause is an organisational or managerial dysfunction.

THE EFFECTS OF STRESS

Stress is a perceived quality. This means that there is no absolute measure of stress, but it is what we think it is. In this respect stress is different from many other illnesses. It cannot be measured objectively by taking someone's temperature or blood pressure. Questionnaires such as the Occupational Stress Indicator[1] provide a structured mechanism for recording how an individual perceives their level of stress, and can be helpful in raising awareness, but they are self-reporting instruments. They depend on honest answers and self-awareness. Stress is personal and, like pain, nobody else can ever really know how badly it affects us or how much suffering it causes. The level of stress that we experience may have little to do with the magnitude of the external pressures and is much more dependent on the way that we react to those pressures. Stress may be in the mind but it has a significant effect on our bodies.

The physiology of stress

We know that the stress process starts with a perceived threat that triggers the flight or fight response. The process is completely automatic and operates under the control of the autonomic nervous system. This is the part of us responsible for maintaining the balance in our bodily functions, such as body temperature, heart rate and digestion. The autonomic nervous system consists of two complementary parts, the sympathetic and the parasympathetic. The sympathetic nervous system is responsible for the flight or fight response and acts to convert stored energy into usable energy. The parasympathetic nervous system reverses this process and is concerned with building up energy stores. The process by which these two branches of the autonomic nervous system balance our bodies is known as homoeostasis. When we interpret a situation as a threat, the brain, acting through the hypothalamus, stimulates the sympathetic nervous system and the pituitary gland.

The chemicals released by this process produce major changes in our bodies. Blood drains away from our extremities and the stomach to increase the supply to our brains and vital organs, while the heart starts to beat faster and blood pressure rises. Our breathing changes and our muscles tense ready for action. The pituitary gland releases a range of hormones that act to maintain performance. The most powerful of these is cortisol which is responsible for keeping high levels of fats and sugars in the bloodstream to provide instant energy. The effect of these biological changes is to switch the body's resources from long term to short term survival. Everything is optimised to overcome the threat. Unfortunately there are no free lunches. Our bodies have to pay the price for the release of energy and resources triggered by the flight or fight response. Fortunately our ancestors developed another set

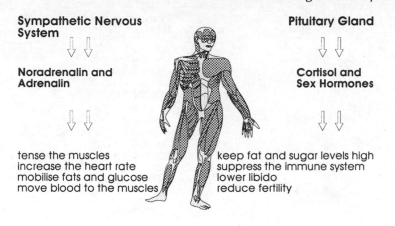

Sympathetic Nervous System

⇓ ⇓

Noradrenalin and Adrenalin

⇓ ⇓

tense the muscles
increase the heart rate
mobilise fats and glucose
move blood to the muscles

Pituitary Gland

⇓ ⇓

Cortisol and Sex Hormones

⇓ ⇓

keep fat and sugar levels high
suppress the immune system
lower libido
reduce fertility

Figure 7: The physiology of stress.

of responses that brought the body back to a normal state of function, and allowed their systems to recover their resources and be ready for the next threat. This process is known as homoeostasis.

Homoeostasis

Under normal circumstances, when the threat has passed, the parasympathetic part of the nervous system operates to return the body to its normal state. The chemical and hormonal changes are reversed, breathing and blood pressure return to normal, blood flows back to the digestive system and so on. The body is once again operating in balance to ensure our long term survival. Homoeostasis is like the operation of a room thermostat, the temperature rises and, at a certain point, the thermostat switches off the heating and the temperature drops. Figure 8 illustrates the changes in the body that occur as a result of homoeostasis.

Most of the time this is exactly what happens. We perceive a threat, the sympathetic nervous system triggers the release of chemicals and hormones into our bloodstream, and our bodies switch into an optimal state. The threat passes and our parasympathetic nervous system returns the body to normal. The potentially harmful changes are reversed and we carry on with our lives. There may have been a short term depletion of some of our long term resources, but no harm is done. However, in the twentieth century, it is not only the nature of the threat that is different, it is also the duration of the threat. If the flight or fight response is constantly

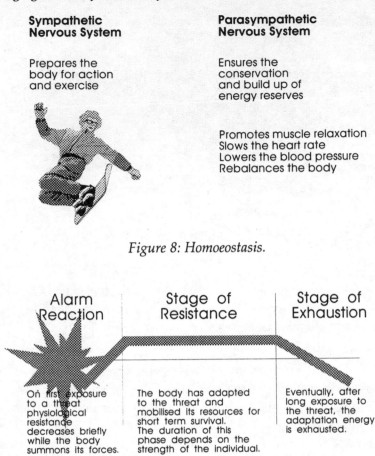

**Sympathetic
Nervous System**

Prepares the
body for action
and exercise

**Parasympathetic
Nervous System**

Ensures the
conservation
and build up of
energy reserves

Promotes muscle relaxation
Slows the heart rate
Lowers the blood pressure
Rebalances the body

Figure 8: Homoeostasis.

Alarm Reaction

On first exposure
to a threat
physiological
resistance
decreases briefly
while the body
summons its forces.

Stage of Resistance

The body has adapted
to the threat and
mobilised its resources for
short term survival.
The duration of this
phase depends on the
strength of the individual.

Stage of Exhaustion

Eventually, after
long exposure to
the threat, the
adaptation energy
is exhausted.

Figure 9: General adaptation syndrome.

being triggered then our bodies never get the chance to return to normal. Eventually we reach a point where we can no longer sustain the imbalance in our body chemistry and we start to become exhausted. Professor Hans Selye[2] described this as the General Adaptation Syndrome and Figure 9 illustrates this process.

As Figure 9 shows, we cannot continue with the chemical and hormonal imbalance for ever. Sooner or later our bodies need to return to normal. If they don't, the chemicals and hormones that helped us to survive in the face of physical danger start to destroy us. With prolonged exposure to continual threats our bodies start to lose the ability to switch on the parasympathetic nervous system and the heightened state, intended only as a response to short term danger, becomes the norm.

It is as if we had turned up the temperature setting on the room thermostat to maximum. Instead of switching on when we need it the heating stays on almost all the time. It is wasteful, unpleasant and may make us ill. After a while we get used to the new temperature and stop thinking about ways of reducing the heating level. We get used to the discomfort and pay the price.

The stress diseases

We have seen that if the threat continues our ability to adapt eventually becomes exhausted and our performance suffers. What happens is that the cortisone, adrenalin and noradrenalin act to increase our blood pressure, blood sugar and blood fats. This produces the following effects:

- increased heart rate;

- increased respiration rate;

- increased blood supply to brain;

- dilated pupils;

- dry mouth;

- sweating;

- reduction in blood supply to less vital organs.

These physical changes, if continued over time, can lead to stress-related illness. Although the relationship between stress and disease is still not fully understood, stress may be a contributory factor in many illnesses including cardiovascular disease and cancer. Professor Cary Cooper et al, in their book *Living with Stress*, list some of the ailments known to have a link to stress:[3]

- hypertension or high blood pressure;

- coronary thrombosis or heart attack;

- migraine;

- hay fever and allergies;

- asthma;

- pruritus or intense itching;
- peptic ulcers;
- constipation;
- colitis;
- rheumatoid arthritis;
- menstrual difficulties;
- nervous dyspepsia or flatulence and indigestion;
- hyperthyroidism or overactive thyroid gland;
- diabetes mellitus;
- skin disorders;
- tuberculosis;
- depression.

The symptoms of stress

As well as understanding the physiology we also need to know how to recognise stress in ourselves and others. To identify stress in ourselves we need to be aware of some of the more common symptoms. Symptoms are what an individual complains of and may not be obvious to other people. Signs are the visible indicators of stress and may not be apparent to the individual suffering from stress. The following list shows some of the more common symptoms of the stress process. The relationship between stress and illness is complex, and is not fully understood. Although the following symptoms have been linked to stress, they are not necessarily a result of stress.

Physical symptoms are as follows:

- altered sleep patterns, for example, difficulty getting to sleep, early waking;
- tiredness;
- lethargy;
- breathlessness, bouts of dizziness, light-headedness;

- indigestion, heartburn;

- nausea;

- bowel disturbance, for example, diarrhoea, constipation;

- headaches;

- muscle tension, for example, neck pain, back pain;

- nervous twitches;

- alteration in habits

  — increase or decrease in eating,

  — increased drinking,

  — loss of sexual drive,

  — increased smoking,

Mental symptoms are as follows:

- irritability and aggression;

- anxiety and apprehension;

- poor decision making;

- preoccupation with trivia;

- inability to prioritise;

- difficulty in coping;

- mood changes and swings;

- difficulty concentrating;

- deterioration in recent memory;

- feelings of failure;

- lack of self-worth;

- isolation.

It is important to recognise the kind of symptoms stress can cause in you. 'Listen' to your body and use the symptoms as a warning that stress may be affecting you.

Signs of stress

Stress affects different people in different ways and there are no clear-cut indicators we can use to identify stress in others. The best we can do is to be sensitive to other people's feelings, and look for changes in appearance, habits and behaviour. The following list describes some of the more common signs of stress.

Altered appearance:

- lack of care in appearance;
- looks miserable;
- looks tired;
- looks nervous or apprehensive;
- looks agitated;

Altered habits:

- eating more, eating less;
- drinking more;
- smoking more;
- increased absence;
- increased accidents;

Altered behaviour:

- irritability;
- aggression;
- mood swings;
- poor concentration;
- poor decision making;
- reduced performance.

This list isn't a complete list of all the signs of stress, but it does indicate some of the more noticeable aspects of stress at work.

Understanding the relationship between pressure and stress helps us to understand what is happening in our bodies when we feel 'stressed'. It is a normal, common, human reaction to a threat.

The key question is how do we manage this reaction to produce positive not negative outcomes. The answer lies in managing the beginning and the end of the stress process. In other words we manage the perception of a threat and we manage the way we adapt to a perceived threat. We can combine these two approaches to turn pressure into peak performance.

The perception of pressure

The General Adaptation Syndrome assumes that each individual will react to a stressful situation in a certain way. It fails to take into account the individual's ability to interpret a threat as a source of pressure and act to change his situation. This aspect of the stress process was addressed in the 1970s by Richard Lazarus. Lazarus defined stress as follows:

> Stress refers to a very broad class of problems differentiated from other problem areas because it deals with any demands which tax the system, whatever it is, a physiological system, a social system, or a psychological system, and the response of that system.[4]

Lazarus said that an individual's stress reaction 'depends on how a person interprets or appraises (consciously or unconsciously) the significance of a harmful, threatening or challenging event'.[5] Lazarus's work extended the concept of stress from a simple, mechanistic response to a threat to one that includes the way the individual interprets the threat. Lazarus changes the emphasis in the stress process from the nature of the threat to the attitude of the individual. It is the way that a threat is perceived by the individual that governs the outcome of the stress process, not the threat itself. Lazarus went on to suggest that the less a person feels they are able to cope with a threat, the more stress they will experience. Lazarus's work suggests that the key elements in the stress process are:

* the way an individual interprets the threat;

* the way an individual perceives their ability to cope.

Professor Cary Cooper, writing in 1978, provides an excellent summary of the factors involved in the stress process.

> 'It can be seen that a particular type of person under pressure from certain kinds of environmental stressors can find himself in a stress state. Whether or not a person will be able to cope will depend

on his perception of threat from the stimuli, his coping capacities, the strength of the stressors and other factors such as his physical and psychological health at the time of the person–environment interaction.'[6]

A year later, Cary Cooper writing with Tom Cummings developed a model showing the stress process as an interaction between an individual and his environment.

- Individuals, for the most part, try to keep their thoughts, emotions and relationships with the world in a 'steady state'.

- Each factor of a person's emotional and physical state has a 'range of stability', in which that person feels comfortable. On the other hand, when forces disrupt one of these factors beyond the range of stability, the individual must act or cope to restore a feeling of comfort.

- An individual's behaviour aimed at maintaining a steady state makes up their 'adjustment process' or coping strategies.

In their article Cummings and Cooper define stress as: 'Any force that puts a psychological or physical factor beyond its range of stability producing a strain within the individual. Knowledge that a stress is likely to occur, constitutes a threat to the individual. A threat can cause a strain because of what it signifies to the person'.[7]

The model of stress based on the relationship between the person and their environment, known as the 'person environment fit', is the one most generally accepted by stress researchers and this model provides the theoretical framework for the positive management of pressure described in this book.

We know from our own experience that this definition makes sense. We may be exposed to the same pressure on different occasions and react in a different way each time. On one occasion a traffic jam may cause stress, the next day we may not even notice the delay. Stress is not a simple mechanistic process in which the same event always produces the same outcome. People are not machines and the laws of mechanics do not apply to human psychology. Cummings and Cooper recognise that it is not the threat that causes stress, it is the perception of the threat. They also suggest that a threat doesn't actually need to occur to cause stress. There is a feedback loop in operation where the stress itself can be the threat. 'Knowledge that a stress is *likely* to occur constitutes a threat to the individual' (my emphasis). This suggests that we do not need an external threat to suffer from stress. To use a somewhat hackneyed phrase, stress really is all in the mind.

'We have nothing to fear but fear itself.' We need to recognise that we can control our response to a threat. We can manage and overcome our fear. Frank Herbert, the author of the classic science fiction novel *Dune*, describes the process for overcoming fear in what he calls 'the response from the Litany against Fear'.

> I must not fear. Fear is the mind-killer. Fear is the little death that brings total obliteration. I will face my fear. I will permit it to pass over me and through me. And when it has gone past I will turn the inner eye to see its path. Where the fear has gone there will be nothing. Only I will remain. (p14)[8]

Perception is our reality. It is important to recognise that stress is about how we see the world, not how the world really is. This difference is fundamental to our ability to manage the stress process.

The four way model of stress

Stress is the outcome of a process that begins with a perceived threat or the possibility of a perceived threat. This perceived threat is pressure. Pressure can come from anywhere. It can be work related, home related, to do with family or friends, or it can be imagined. Pressure can be a major event or a trivial, inconsequential occurrence. Pressure is idiosyncratic and the events that cause pressure for you may not cause pressure for me. Stress occurs when the perceived pressure on an individual exceeds that individual's perceived ability to cope.

This definition contains five key words: pressure, individual, coping, stress and perceived. Stress is about balance. Our lives are in balance when our perceived coping skills, our ability to adapt, are greater than the pressure upon us. Our perception of pressure, our capacity for managing pressure and whether we tend to be stress prone or stress resistant are all influenced by our personality. Figure 10 is a simplified, mechanistic model of the stress process. It shows the interdependency of the four components and the relationship between them.

The model shows that the effects of stress are determined by the force exerted by pressure counterbalanced by the coping skills. In

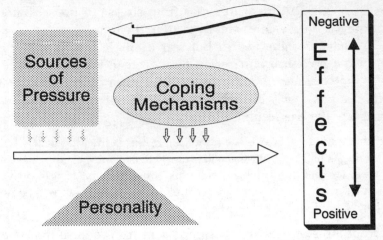

Figure 10: The four-way stress model.

the above diagram an increase in the amount of pressure will tip the pointer upwards and produce more negative effects. A reduction in the amount of pressure will have the opposite effect.

Personality acts as a moderator or an amplifier for the stress process. Figure 11 shows the influence of personality type on the

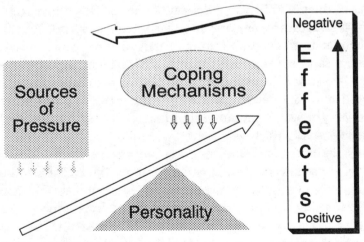

Figure 11: The stress-prone four-way model.

effects of stress. A stress-prone personality is illustrated by moving the pivot to the right. In this case a small amount of pressure will produce large negative effects. A hardy, stress resistant personality has the effect of moving the pivotal point to the left. When this

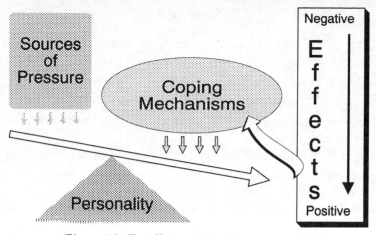

Figure 12: Excellent coping four-way model.

happens more force is required to tip the pointer upwards.

Pressure is counterbalanced by coping mechanisms. A wide range of well-developed coping mechanisms will outweigh the pressure and reduce the negative effects. This is shown in Figure 12.

The models show the effect of differences in the sources of pressure, personality and coping mechanisms on the outcome of the stress process. The arrow at the top of figures 10 and 11 shows the way in which the negative effects of stress can create additional pressure. Stress is cumulative and can itself be a source of pressure. Pressure can thus build into a negative downward spiral where stress becomes self-generating. The inability to cope leads to self-doubt and a lack of confidence. Perception is altered so that trivial incidents are blown up out of all proportion and this vicious circle continues until the individual breaks down. In figure 12, the process is different. The positive effects of pressure, the 'feeling good' factors, add to the perceived coping skills and strengthen the individual's ability to manage pressure. In this situation there is a positive, upward spiral of increased resourcefulness. Success creates success.

Managing pressure means managing all the stress-producing factors: perception, pressure, personality and coping. Chapter 3 describes the behaviours that help an individual to manage pressure. Chapter 4 looks at the way our freedom to choose changes the perception of pressure and the remaining chapters explore a variety of coping mechanisms.

References

1   Cooper, C L, Sloan, S and Williams, S (1988) *The Occupational Stress Indicator:* NFER Nelson, Windsor.
2   Selye, H (1946) 'The General Adaption Syndrome and the Diseases of Adaptation' *Journal of Clinical Endocrinogy* 6: 117.
3   Cooper, C L, Cooper R D, Eaker, L H (1988) *Living with Stress:* Penguin, London.
4   Lazarus, R S (1971) 'The Concepts of Stress and Disease' in L Levi (ed) *Society, Stress and Disease* Vol 1, pp53-60: Oxford University Press, London.
5   Lazarus, R S (1976) *Patterns of Adjustment:* McGraw-Hill, New York.
6   Cooper C L (1978) 'Work Stress', in P Warr (ed) *Psychology at Work:* Penguin, London.
7   Cummings, T, Cooper C L (1979) 'A Cybernetic Framework for the Study of Occupational Stress' *Human Relations* 32: 395-419.
8   Herbert, F (1966) *'Dune':* Victor Gollanz Ltd, London.

3
Managing Behaviour

I first met Michael four years ago when he was working as the production manager of a metal fabrications company. He came into the meeting with an aggressive, almost hostile attitude. He sat down and stared at me across the table, put his pack of cigarettes and lighter in front of him, crossed his arms in front of his chest and said he hoped this wouldn't take long because he had a lot to do. Michael was 38 but looked 50. He had started work at 5.00 that morning and wouldn't go home until after 7.00 pm. Michael usually worked a 12 to 15 hour day, 6 days a week. His first marriage had ended in divorce.

I got to know Michael quite well over the next few years. He was a likeable, forthright person who put an enormous amount of effort into everything he did. He was proud of the fact that he worked longer and harder than anyone else, and firmly believed in leading by example. He would think nothing of getting up in the early hours of the morning to drive several hundred miles to visit a customer or a supplier and never seemed able to take a holiday. On the few occasions when he took time off, he rang the office several times a day, just to check everything was all right. Michael took his work very seriously, was proud of his achievements and had the respect of his staff.

After a couple of years Michael became the production director and continued to work at his usual rate. A number of people, including the managing director, tried to get him to slow down a bit, take more time off and warned him that he couldn't carry on like this for ever. Michael just laughed it off and said he was fine. He was absolutely convinced that there was nothing wrong in working flat out for 80 to 100 hours a week.

A year ago, Michael's company hit major problems. It made a lot of people redundant and was sold to a competitor. Michael became the managing director and, as you would expect, worked with even more energy and vigour than he had before. Or at least he did until a month ago. It appears that Michael wasn't invulnerable after all. He died of a heart attack, aged 42, while driving to a meeting.

We are all different. To quote Ralph Waldo Emerson, 'We boil at different degrees.' Individual differences in personality and behaviour influence our perception of a threat and our ability to adapt to pressure. Under the same pressure someone will respond positively, someone negatively and someone else will have no reaction. When we understand why some people thrive on pressure while others fall apart, we can start to modify our behaviour to produce a positive response. This chapter explores the three key aspects of personality that influence the outcome of the stress process. These are Type A behaviour, control and influence, and Hardiness.

TYPE A BEHAVIOUR

The concept of Type A behaviour was discovered in the early 1960s by two American cardiologists, Meyer Friedman and Ray Rosenman, working with a biochemist called Sanford Beyers. They wanted to know if the way someone felt or thought had any influence on the development of coronary heart disease. In their early research, the team interviewed several hundred people; mainly business managers and heart specialists. Over 70 per cent of these people thought that stress at work, combined with a competitive personality, seemed to precipitate heart attacks. Friedman and Rosenman then set up a research project to investigate the relationship between emotional stress and heart disease. They discovered a set of behaviours that seemed to characterise people at risk from heart disease and called this Type A behaviour.

Friedman and Rosenman defined Type A behaviour in their book, *Type A Behaviour and Your Heart,* as: 'An action-emotion complex that can be observed in any person who is aggressively involved in a chronic, incessant struggle to achieve more and more in less and less time and, if required to do so, against the opposing efforts of other things or persons'.[1]

They also listed the following Type A characteristics:

Possessing the habit of explosively accentuating various key words in ordinary speech without real need and tending to utter the last few words of sentences far more rapidly than the opening words.

Always moving, walking and eating rapidly.

Feeling an impatience with the rate at which most events take place.

Attempting to do two or more things at the same time, for example driving your car and dictating letters, thinking about another subject while someone else is talking to you, signing letters while talking to someone on the phone and so on.

Finding it difficult to talk about things which don't have a personal interest.

Always feeling guilty when attempting to relax.

Trying to schedule more into less and less time, and making few allowances for the unexpected events.

Having a chronic sense of time urgency.[2]

In the same book Friedman and Rosenman also described the opposite of Type A behaviour and called this Type B. The Type B person is someone who is:

completely free of all the habits and exhibiting none of the traits of the Type A personality, doesn't suffer from impatience and time urgency, has no need to impress others with their achievements, plays games in order to find relaxation and fun – not to demonstrate their ability to win and are able to work without agitation and relax without guilt.[3]

Other researchers have subsequently modified the concept of Type A behaviour by explaining it in terms of styles of coping with the uncontrollable[4] and a person's basic belief systems.[5] These ideas complement the original concept of Type A and provide a composite picture of a Type A person as someone who is competitive, hard driving, tense, aggressive, preoccupied with deadlines, work oriented and with a high need to control their environment.

Type A behaviour is highly regarded in the Western world. Many successful people demonstrate some, if not most, of the above behaviours, particularly attempting to do several things at once. Friedman and Rosenman describe this 'polyphasic' activity as one of the most common traits of the Type A person. Many managers and senior executives, together with almost every member of the boards of some of our most successful companies, appear to be Type A. Recruitment and promotion systems tend to reward Type A behaviour, and interviewers see some of these traits as positive indicators of success.

Type B people seem to be more able to cope with pressure than Type As. Perhaps this is because they are less competitive and less worried about the consequences or have a lower need for achievement. Type Bs are also less likely to suffer from work overload than Type As and may not 'push themselves' as hard. However, there is little evidence to suggest that the widespread belief that Type A people are better performers than Type B is valid. A study of 355 life insurance agents found similar performance levels between Type As and Type Bs with the Type As reporting more health complaints.[6] Managers should not therefore assume that Type A behaviour means high performance.

Type As have a tendency to over-commit. They are competitive and ambitious, and they don't like to say no. They create their own pressure by failing to recognise when to slow down or stop. A high Type A is like a juggler who keeps taking on more and more balls because they can't say no. They can manage three or four without any problems, five or six are a struggle, and if they continue to accept more they run the risk of dropping them all. Type As need to learn to say NO!

Type A and heart disease

The negative aspect of Type A behaviour is that although it is commonly associated with success in business, it is also regarded by some researchers as a major contributory factor to heart disease. In the UK, heart disease is the largest cause of death for men aged between 35 and 50. In 1992, heart disease accounted for almost a third of all male deaths and 27 per cent of all female deaths.[7] This doesn't mean that Type A behaviour causes heart disease, but there is evidence to suggest that it can be a contributory factor.[8]

Recent research into the relationship between Type A behaviour and heart disease suggests that, despite over 30 years of study, it is still not possible to claim that there is an identifiable pattern of coronary-prone behaviour. It seems that there may be a pattern of behaviour that predicts heart disease but more research needs to be done. The good news is that the attention given to Type A behaviour has produced some benefit. In the words of D W Johnston, summarising the current status of Type A behaviour research:

> While there has been little increase in understanding of the role and behavioural factors in Coronary Heart Disease, as a result of this 30 years of endeavour there have been clinical benefits. It has clearly been shown that what are regarded as coronary prone behaviours can readily be modified and that their modification appears to confer some health benefits and no detectable health hazards.[9]

Taking a global view of Type A behaviour may not, therefore, be the most accurate predictor of stress or subsequent health problems. One way of understanding the impact of Type A behaviour on health is to look at two contrasting sub-components of Type A Behaviour:

- the achievement-striving pattern;
- the impatient-irritability pattern.

A person with the achievement-striving pattern is someone who is concerned with success. They are focused on achieving results, and their Type A behaviour is competitive and produces successful outcomes. They push themselves hard but do so in a positive direction and have learnt to channel their Type A behaviour into successful projects. The impatience-irritability pattern is more worrying. This pattern is a characteristic of someone whose Type A behaviour never seems to produce successful outcomes. They become angry and frustrated because things don't happen they way they want them to happen or they feel they have lost control. These characteristics have also been linked to 'free floating' hostility. People who take a hostile approach to the world and do not seem to have anything specific to direct their hostility towards may also be more at risk from heart disease.[10]

Negative Type A Positive Type A

**Impatience
Irritability** **Achievement
Striving**

Figure 13: Type A behaviours.

Although the research into the relationship between stress, personality type and illness is complex and somewhat confusing, there is evidence to suggest that stress is a contributory factor in many illnesses, and that personality type can act either as a moderator or an amplifier in the stress process. Factors such as grief, hostility, social isolation, fear and work demands have all been implicated in heart disease independently of Type A behaviour.[11] Common sense suggests that reacting to a particular event in a calm, controlled, confident manner is better for us than panicking, becoming irritable and impatient, and feeling unable to cope. Someone whose behaviour leads to success is more likely to be healthier and more able to manage pressure than someone with the same behaviour who constantly fails to achieve their goals.

CONTROL AND INFLUENCE

The second aspect of behavioural style that influences our response to pressure is the extent to which we feel in control or can influence events.

Imagine two people working at a computer typing-in information. They are employed in data preparation work, keying in names and addresses for a direct mail company. One is a self-employed sub-contractor, the other works as a data entry clerk for a large computer company.

One of them sits in a pleasant study, looking out over the moors. He is casually dressed, has a cup of coffee by his side and music playing in the background. The house is full of the smell of baking bread that he put into the oven before sitting down to work. He is completely in control of his working environment. He can work when he wants for as long as he wants, provided he finishes the project when he said he would.

The other man sits in a large, open plan office. He is wearing a suit and tie, and sitting looking at a blank white wall. He is working at a similar machine doing a similar job, but he has had to log on in the morning and the supervisor program monitors his key stroke rate. He has to work at the average rate of 100 key presses a minute and warning messages flash if he works too slowly. He needs to ask the supervisor if he wants a break and the machine times his absence. If he's away too long it goes on his work record and he may lose his job.

This is an extreme example of the difference between internal and external locus of control. Internal control is when you feel that you make things happen. External control is when things happen to you. It's the difference between managing your life and having it managed for you. The first man has internal control. He decides when he works and how he works, he makes the decisions and actively manages his working environment. The second man has external control. He has no influence over how he works or when and where he works. He is unable to decide or change anything and is managed by his environment. The funny thing is, both men produce exactly the same results.

Most of us are in jobs that give us some opportunity to control our environment, but for much of the time we are controlled by others. Lack of control and influence is a major cause of stress at work, and is one of the chief reasons why stress affects blue collar and clerical workers more than managers. At its worst, lack of control is powerlessness. Think back to the flight or fight response and imagine the terror of being trapped, paralysed with fear and the utter frustration of not being able to do anything to change the outcome of a negative event.

Locus of control

The concept of locus of control was introduced by an American psychologist, Julian Rotter, in the 1960s.[12] Locus of control refers to the beliefs that individuals have about the extent to which they control events or events control them. People who believe that they are able to control and influence events have an internal locus of control. They are 'internals'. People who think that things happen to them and they are powerless to influence them have external control. They are 'externals'. The relationship between control and stress is summarised as: 'To the extent to which an individual judges himself to have control or mastery in a situation, the probability is that he will be less likely to perceive a situation as threatening or stress inducing, and in turn, less likely to manifest adverse reaction patterns' (p 94.)[13] This definition suggests that people who have internal control are less likely to feel the effects of the stress process because they believe that they can control what happens to them. Those with external control feel helpless and therefore become more stressed.

The understanding of locus of control and its relation to stress has been refined by introducing the concept that it is the difference between the amount of control individuals think they should have and the amount of control they actually have that causes the stress reaction. For example, somebody who believes that he has internal control will feel under stress when faced with a situation where he is unable to exercise any influence. Similarly, someone who believes that things happen to her may find herself under stress when she's forced to choose or is in a position to influence the outcome of an event. People with an external locus of control may find their life is far easier if they just let other people tell them what to do or make their decisions for them. Externals perceive a threat and feel under pressure when they have to start using their own judgements.

As with the Type A, B dimension locus of control is not an either/or state but a continuum. Everyone has some elements of internal and external control, just as we all have aspects of Type A and Type B behaviours.

A person's belief in whether they have internal or external control is a deep rooted belief that has developed over many years. It is not a transitory characteristic that can be changed overnight. However, in learning to manage pressure in a rapidly changing world, we need to improve our ability to influence events around us.

We can take two different approaches to improving our perceived control. The first is a 'bury your head in the sand' approach. This means structuring your life in such a way that you don't have to accept any responsibility for your behaviours. In a work setting, this may mean finding yourself in a job where you're comfortable working for an autocratic manager. You are told what to do and you get on with it. At home you may let your partner or your friends make all the decisions for you. American author Luke Rhinehart took the concept of abnegating responsibility to its extreme in his novel, *The Dice Man*.[14] The protagonist, a bored New York psychiatrist, lets the roll of a die make all his decisions for him. At first he rolls the dice to make trivial decisions, later the dice rule his life and, freed from personal responsibility, he 'rampages from one outrage to the next'. According to Rhinehart, 'The secret of successful dicelife is to be a puppet on the strings of the die.'

The other approach is to manage your life actively. Decide what you want and take control of your destiny. This is the path to personal excellence and peak performance. You may encounter more pressure but the results will be worth it.

Taking control

We need to analyse the situation and decide whether or not we can influence the outcome. We need to learn to differentiate between the things we can do something about and those things beyond our control. When we can do this we stop ourselves from worrying about things we can't influence and concentrate on doing something about the things we can.

In our experience of working with people at all levels in a large number of organisations, we have found that no one is in a job that is so tightly controlled and managed that they cannot increase the amount of influence that they can assert, even if only marginally. Take, for example, somebody working on a till at a supermarket. Most of their working day will be strictly governed by the needs of the store and the demands of the customers. However, there may be opportunities to exert some influence over the way in which they deal with customers, organise rotas, operate till procedures and so on. Each of these initiatives may, in themselves, be inconsequential. However, together they can help someone to feel slightly more in control of their working environment.

It is not necessary to have complete autonomy or make a radical change in our ability to control our work. Small changes can be enough to shift the focus from external to internal control. As soon as you start doing something you start taking control. The more you're able to influence events around you, the more capable and in control you feel. This is obviously much easier in some jobs than others but it's worth thinking carefully about your own situation and identifying an area in which you can start being more influential.

The consequences of stress and lack of control

The consequence of an event influences the extent to which lack of control causes stress. Being stuck in a traffic jam, for example, may be irritating but it may be relatively unimportant. It may delay you getting to work by a few minutes or half an hour, but no real damage will be done. Although you may get frustrated and impatient the stress, if any, will be relatively minor. The situation is different when you have an important job interview, a key presentation to a client or a major meeting. The pressure is greater because the consequences are greater. Common sense tells us that we make better plans and exercise more control when we are concerned about the consequences of failure. We take more care to avoid a delay on a journey to catch a plane than we do on a journey to the supermarket.

THE HARDY PERSONALITY

The third aspect of individual differences is the Hardy personality. In an attempt to explain why some people became ill as a result of stress while others thrived, Suzannne Kobasa, a psychologist from New York University, developed the concept of the 'Hardy personality'. The Hardy personality is centred on the concept of control and influence, and the feeling of being in charge. It embodies the principles of actively managing pressure and being in a resourceful state.

The Hardy personality theory states that: 'among persons facing significant stressors, those high in hardiness will be significantly less likely to fall ill, either mentally or physically than those who lack hardness or who display alienation, powerlessness and threat in the face of change'.[15] Kobasa and her colleagues wanted to know what was different about some people that allowed them to stay healthy under pressure. Her researchers studied several hundred managers over a five-year period and tried to answer the key question, 'Is there something that differentiates the high stress–low illness group from the high stress–high illness group?'

Kobasa found three characteristics that differentiated the groups; commitment, control and challenge. She described commitment as 'the ability to believe in the truth, importance and interest of who one is and what one is doing and, thereby, the tendency to involve oneself fully in the many situations of life, including work, family, interpersonal relationships and social institutions'. Control is defined as the 'tendency to believe and act as if one can influence the course of events. Persons with control seek explanations for why something is happening with emphasis on their own responsibility and not in terms of other actions or fate'. Control in this context is the same concept as locus of control described earlier in this chapter. Hardy people have internal control. The third characteristic, challenge, is based on the individual's belief that 'change, rather than stability, is the normative mode of life'. Challenge means that an individual looks for stimulation and change, and can tolerate uncertainty.

Kobasa *et al* summarised the kind of person who can deal with extended pressure without suffering from the effects of stress as someone who must:

> be aware of and involved with oneself, believe he can control and
> transform the events of his experience, and perceive change as an
> opportunity and challenge rather than threat. The longer one has
> this overall orientation, the greater will be his accumulated skills
> and resources for dealing with stress. When stress does occur,
> he will be energised and exhilarated rather than debilitated and
> worried.[16]

The opposite of the Hardy personality is the stress-prone or vulnerable person. This is someone who doesn't feel in control and suffers stress from small amounts of pressure.

MANAGING CHANGE

Change is a threat or an opportunity. It all depends on how we look at it. A recent poll[17] showed that 99 per cent of *The Times* 1000 companies are going through major change. We cannot avoid change; it is an inevitable part of life. But, change is changing. Professor Charles Handy, writing in *The Age of Unreason*,[18] says that change is not what it used to be. Handy believes that the future is fundamentally different from the past and that we need to change our way of thinking to manage this 'discontinuous' change. Handy's argument is based on three assumptions.

> That the changes are different this time: they are discontinuous and not part of a pattern; that such discontinuity happens from time to time in history although it is confusing and disturbing, particularly to those in power.

> That it is the little changes which can in fact make the biggest differences to our lives, even if these go unnoticed at the time, and that it is the changes in the way our work is organised which will make the biggest differences to the way we will live.

> That discontinuous change requires discontinuous upside-down thinking to deal with it, even if both thinkers and thoughts appear absurd at first sight.

Handy illustrates his theme with a story about a frog. If you put a frog in a pan of cold water and slowly heat the water, the frog, although it could jump out at any time, will remain in the pan. The frog will let itself be boiled alive. It is too comfortable. It is, in Handy's words; 'too comfortable with continuity to realise that continuous change at some point becomes discontinuous and demands a change in behaviour'. We are reluctant to accept that we have to change but we need to recognise that the world is different and, unless we want to end up like the frog, we have to adapt to changing circumstances.

People fear change most when it challenges their security and when what they have is put at risk. Worrying about change is being afraid of the unknown. It is going into situations without being prepared for what to expect. Many people working in organisations that are going through major changes know that change is going to take place. They realise that life is going to be different but they do not know how it's going to be different and may come to doubt their ability to survive in the new world. In many ways the threat of change is worse than the change itself. We have no control over the unknown and this lack of control cuts right through us.

Rosabeth Moss Kanter, one of the leading writers on organisational change, supports this view when she writes about how American managers see change as a threat: 'They feel at the mercy of change or the threat of change in a world marked by turbulence, uncertainty and instability, because their comfort, let alone their success, is dependent on many decisions of many players they can barely, if at all, influence'.[19]

The hardiness characteristics of commitment, control and challenge are all mechanisms for managing change to produce peak performance. When we look forward to change as a challenge our perception alters and we see it as an opportunity, not a threat. In order to manage change we need to alter our thinking. As Handy says, 'Discontinuous change requires discontinuous upside-down thinking'. We need to see change as the norm, and understand that the only way that we can deal with rapid change is by being flexible, responsive and determined.

Control is the key to managing change. You cannot manage pressure unless you're in control. Discontinuous change creates a world of opportunity for those people who enthusiastically embrace change. If nothing changes, there is no opportunity and no room for growth or development. Learning to live with change involves taking risks and being prepared to accept an occasional failure as the price you pay for trying. People who believe that change is the natural order of things do not need the security of maintaining the status quo and look forward to the world tomorrow being different from the world today. These are the people who thrive on change and, as a result, shape the future.

The first and most fundamental choice you have to make about managing change is to decide who you want to manage your life. If the answer is *you* then you should make sure that you stay in control. Continue to make positive choices. Continue to decide the things you will do, and when and how you will do them. Be prepared for the unexpected, overcome setbacks and failures, and react positively and flexibly to ever-changing circumstances. Live the life you want, not the life you're given.

References

1   Friedman, M, Rosenman, R H (1974) *Type A Behaviour and Your Heart:* Knopf, New York.
2   Friedman, M, Rosenman, R H, op cit.
3   Friedman, M, Rosenman, R H, op cit.
4   Glass, D C (1977) *Behaviour Patterns, Stress and Coronary Disease:* Erlbaum, Hillsdale, N J.
5   Price, V A (1982) *Type A Behaviour Pattern:* Academic Press, New York.
6   Matteson, M T, Ivancevitch, J M and Smith, S V (1984) 'Relation of Type A Behaviour to Performance and Satisfaction among Sales Personnel' *Journal of Vocational Behaviour* 25: 203-14.
7   Source: Office of Population, Census and Surveys (OPCS) statistics.
8   Sales, S M (1969) 'Differences among Individuals in Affective Behavioural Biochemical and Physiological Responses to Variations in Workload' PhD Thesis, University of Michigan.
9   Johnston, D W (1993) 'The Current Status of the Coronary Prone Behaviour Pattern' *Journal of Research in Social Medicine,* July, 86: 406-9.
10 Smith, T W (1992) 'Hostility and Health: Current Status of a Psychosomatic Hypothesis' *Health Psychology* 11(3):139-50.
11 Conduit, E H (1992) 'If A-B does not predict heart disease, why bother with it? A Clinician's View' *British Journal of Medical Psychology,* September (3):289-96.
12 Rotter, J B (1966) 'Generalised Expectancies for Internal versus External Control of Reinforcement' *Psychology Monograph,* 80.
13 Chan, K B (1977) 'Individual Differences in Reactions to Stress and their Personality and Situational Determinance' *Social Science and Medicine* 11:89-103.
14 Rhinehart, L (1972) *The Dice Man:* Panther, ceased publishing, this title is now available from Harper Collins.
15 Kobasa, S C (1985) *Conceptualisation and Measurement of Personality in Job Stress Research,* NIOSH Symposium, Measures of Job Stress Workshop, New Orleans, 21-3 October.
16 Kobasa, S C, Hilker, R R J and Maddi S R (1980) 'Remaining Healthy in the Encounter with Stress', in *Stress, Work, Health:* American Medical Association, Chicago.
17 MORI Poll (1994) commissioned by TDA Consulting Group.

18 Handy, C (1989) *The Age of Unreason:* Business Books, London.
19 Kanter, R M (1981) *The Change Masters; Corporate Entrepreneurs at Work* (p 62): George Allen & Unwin, London.

Part 2
Action

4

Positive Choices

I enjoyed Pete's visits. He was always friendly and enthusiastic, and had a no-nonsense, decisive, 'can do' attitude. I never saw Pete angry or upset and even when things didn't quite go according to plan he seemed able to find something good about the situation. Pete was one of those people who didn't seem to have a care in the world. He always had time to talk, and inspired trust and confidence.

I used to wonder what it was about Pete that made people feel good when he was around. He wasn't particularly extroverted. He didn't tell a lot of jokes. He was just good company. I finally realised it was because he was always positive and always seemed in control. Pete taught me that being in control starts with positive choices. You shape the world into your own image and the more positive you are the more the world becomes the way you want it. It is the difference between drifting along, taking life as it comes, and deciding that every day is going to be a good day and making it happen.

Pete showed me that whether a day is good or bad doesn't depend on what happens, it depends on how you see the day.

The difference between stress and growth is successful coping. It is not how well we cope that matters but how well we *think* we can cope. Positive thinking produces positive coping. This chapter is about taking control of our lives and actively shaping our future. Understanding provides the framework for action but we need to take action to improve our ability to manage pressure. Action has to be directed. It has to have a purpose. Unless the things we do produce the results we want there is no point in doing them. We have to start by knowing what we want from our lives. If we don't know what we want we have little chance of getting it and no opportunity to plan for it. In the words of Lewis Carroll:

> 'Would you tell me, please, which way I ought to go from here?'
> 'That depends a good deal on where you want to get to,' said the cat.
> 'I don't much care where,' said Alice.
> 'Then it doesn't matter which way you go,' said the cat.

MAKING A CHOICE

We manage pressure for a purpose. A balanced life is a trade-off between doing the things we want to do and doing the things we have to do in order to do the things we want to do. We need to direct energy into activities that give us the things we want. If we want to spend more time with the family there is no sense in continuing to work a 60-hour week. If we want promotion, money or status then we direct our energy into work and shouldn't complain about not having enough time for the family. Often we want the best of both worlds, and don't appreciate the cost to ourselves and our families of trying to balance conflicting priorities. Conflicting goals produce stress. Stress disappears when our desires, our behaviours and our abilities are in harmony.

Deciding your goals means thinking about your values. What do you *really* want out of life? Is it health and happiness, a big house, a fast car, lots of children, good holidays, financial security? Achieving the right balance between the things you want and the price you are prepared to pay for them is very personal. There are no right answers and you can be the only judge. Managing pressure is concerned with the mismatch between what you want and what you get. In Chapter 5 we look in more detail at managing your priorities. For now, the issue is the extent to which you are satisfied with what you are doing. If you are working a 70-hour week because you want to work a 70-hour week, then it's your choice. If you want to work a 30-hour week and find yourself working 70 hours because you feel you have to, then you are under pressure. You have to choose whether the benefits you are getting from working a 70-hour week are worth the discomfort you feel because you are not doing what you want. Is there a point at which you can balance out these two conflicting demands?

The other reason for clarifying your goals is that your ability to achieve peak performance is directly related to the clarity of your goals. Anthony Robbins, writing in *Unlimited Power*,[1] quotes a study of Yale graduates. In 1953 a group of researchers interviewed a number of graduates and asked them if they had a set of clear specific goals written down and with a plan for achieving those goals. Only 3 per cent of the graduates had written goals. The researchers went back in 1973 and interviewed the surviving members of the 1953 class and discovered that the 3 per cent with written goals were worth more in financial terms than the remaining 97 per cent put together. It could be argued that financial worth is not a true measure of success; however, the researchers found that the 3 per cent with written goals seemed on subjective measures to be happier and more content than those without written goals.

BELIEVING IN SUCCESS

Peak performance is a state of mind. It occurs when your mind and body are functioning at their highest level, and you are in your most resourceful, positive and committed state. All of us have achieved things in our lives that we thought were impossible and know the feeling of being at a peak state. Unfortunately, we may only operate at that peak state for short periods of time, maybe once a month, once a year or once every few years. Most of the time we just carry on as normal. We have some good days and some bad days; days when things seem to go right and days when everything seems to go wrong; days when we feel proud of ourselves and days when we feel disappointed. The reasons why we have good and bad days are varied and complex. However, bad days are not inevitable. There is no fundamental law of nature that says people have to have a bad day. We are responsible for the quality of our lives and the goodness of our days. We don't have to feel bad. No matter what happens to us we can find something to take pride in, even if it's only how well we faced adversity.

In his seminars, Tony Robbins gets the audience to think about 'What could you do if you absolutely knew you couldn't fail?' Think about that for a moment. What would you do if you knew you couldn't fail? 'If you were absolutely certain of success, what activities would you pursue, what actions would you take?'[2] If you absolutely knew that you couldn't fail there would be no stress. You would meet every challenge in a positive, enthusiastic and welcoming manner. It would be impossible to perceive of any event as a threat because the outcomes would be positive.

This approach is not meant to be a recommendation for blind faith, foolhardy optimism or living in a Walter Mitty, make-believe world. It is designed to illustrate the power of the mind in influencing the outcome of an event by changing the perception of the event.

LOOKING AT THINGS DIFFERENTLY

We can choose how we perceive pressure. We do not have to accept events as problems. To manage pressure we need to manage the way we interpret events. We need to question our assumptions and, if we are able to identify any specific areas, incidents or events that cause pressure, we should try and seek alternative explanations or interpretations for that event. We need to develop the skill of reframing and of looking at things a different way.

Two people look at a wine glass; one says that it's half full, the other that it's half empty. They are both right but the language they choose to describe the event is very revealing. A few years ago two of my friends were telling me about their problems getting home after a weekend away.

They both had to travel about 100 miles and, by a strange coincidence, both had engine faults. The first friend told me how unlucky he had been, the engine was overheating and he just managed to get home before it gave up completely. It was 'typical of his bad luck'. My other friend had an almost identical experience. He had carburettor problems and only just managed to make it home. He rang to tell me how lucky he'd been. 'The car kept on stopping and we were really lucky to get home before it fell apart.' The events are the same. The perception of the event is completely different.

One interpretation is positive and stress reducing, while the other is negative and stress inducing. Changing the way we look at the world makes an enormous difference to the way we manage pressure. We don't need to prepare for it, we don't need to practice,

Figure 14: Looking at things differently.

we just need to look at things differently. Like looking at Figure 14, when we see the picture change from an old woman to a young lady, we see it in a flash. It may take some effort to see it but, once we do, that's it. In any situation we can look for and find the positive. When we see it, pressure is reduced.

The old saying that every cloud has a silver lining is true; you just need to know where to look. By restating the problem, by looking at things in a different way, we can minimise or eliminate the sources of pressure. We may, for example, be faced with an impossible deadline that we feel unable to meet. Worrying about not being able to meet the deadline is a major source of pressure and our inability to cope with that pressure causes us to suffer from stress. By questioning the reasons for the deadline, we may find that the problem disappears or that what's needed is nowhere near as difficult to produce as we thought.

RESOURCEFULNESS

We have seen that stress is caused by the perception of a threat, or the possibility of a threat, and that the more resourceful we are and the better our coping mechanisms, the more likely we are to achieve a positive outcome from pressure. The best way to manage pressure is therefore to be in a peak state when you are exposed to pressure. If someone wants to push me over they will find it easy when I'm not expecting the push or if they catch me off balance. If I know the push is coming and have taken up a strong, stable stance, they will find it difficult, if not impossible, to push me over. This is stating the obvious but it needs to be said. Pressure at work or at home has a habit of catching us off balance. It comes when we least expect it and it can strike when we are least able to cope. Our ability to handle pressure is directly proportional to our feeling of resourcefulness. The more resourceful we are the easier it gets. When we meet a problem we want to be prepared and not caught unawares.

In managing pressure for peak performance we have two separate and distinct forces operating. We have the perception of pressure as a positive opportunity, not as a threat. This force stops stress occurring because we simply don't perceive a threat and the stress process has nowhere to start. The second element is that the more effectively we manage pressure, the more our performance increases and the stronger our resourceful state becomes. We therefore create an upwards spiral where peak performance increases our ability to manage pressure which, in turn, leads to even more enhanced performance. This positive cycle can continue indefinitely and is the opposite of the burnout cycle described in Chapter 1.

CHOOSING WHEN TO WORRY

One of the key skills in managing pressure is being able to recognise the difference between those things we can control and those things over which we have no control, and act accordingly. If we're stuck in stationary traffic on a motorway, there is nothing we can do to make the traffic move more quickly. There is therefore no point in getting upset or worried about the delay. If it's possible to do something constructive like use a carphone to ring ahead and explain that we're going to be late, or get out some papers to do some work, then we can turn the delay into an opportunity. If it is not possible or appropriate to do something useful then try and find something in the situation that you can enjoy. It may be listening to the radio, looking at the scenery, thinking about something that you haven't had time for, or whatever. Remember; there are no problems, just opportunities in disguise.

Knowing when to worry

Recognising that there are some things over which we have no control does not mean that we have to accept the situation, whatever happens. In deciding not to let the traffic jam upset us or cause us stress, we have taken the decision and we are in control. The decision hasn't been taken for us and we haven't just blindly accepted that we can't do anything about it.

The difference between actively deciding not to do something and passively assuming that we can't do it is fundamental to managing pressure. There are no half-way measures. We are either in control of our own lives or we are not. We make the decisions. We take control.

BREAKING PATTERNS

To achieve peak performance we start by changing our belief systems. Examine what you think and believe about yourself, recognise self-limiting beliefs and discard them. One of the most effective ways of changing your belief systems is to break the patterns. We all get trapped into certain ways of thinking. We believe, perhaps because we've been taught from a very early age, there are some things that we simply can't do. Often these beliefs have no basis in fact, but can be so deeply ingrained that they become self-fulfilling.

Self-limiting beliefs

Think about a little girl coming downstairs one evening for a glass of water and hearing her mother talk to a friend on the phone saying, 'Amy is not very good at maths, she has lots of problems and just can't seem to get the hang of it. Sarah's the smart one, she just seems to be able to do it naturally.' A week later Amy may be told off by her teacher for making careless mistakes in her maths work. Amy may then start to believe that she can't do maths and, now she is aware of her 'problem', she finds herself noticing other comments about her lack of mathematical ability. Throughout her teenage years and her adult life, she finds maths difficult and tries to avoid getting herself into situations where she has to be numerate. Those early comments formed the basis of a self-fulfilling prophecy that may have nothing at all to do with Amy's mathematical ability.

The seeds of self-doubt, self-limiting beliefs and low self-esteem are sown at a very early age, and can be real barriers to achieving peak performance. These beliefs become ingrained and are hard to change. The solution is to replace the limiting beliefs with a belief that people can do anything they want to do and that you are capable of achieving everything you set out to do. The only way to do this is to tell yourself regularly, repeatedly and sincerely. You don't have to convince anyone else, only yourself, and, because we act according to our beliefs about ourselves, our ability will change to reflect our changed beliefs.

REINFORCE SUCCESS

Positive thinking reinforces internal control. We need to improve our self-image and move along the upward spiral of positive reinforcement. Success breeds success. The more we achieve, the more we are capable of achieving. This applies to all areas of our lives. The world of work rewards positive, success-oriented individuals who get on and get things done, and these people, the peak performers, tend to have a positive approach to life. This is also true outside of work. The more positive we are, the more positive we become.

Unfortunately, the way we are brought up and the way we are treated by organisations tend to reinforce the negatives rather than encourage positives. In most organisations, people are quick to point out weaknesses and slow to acknowledge strengths. We can't rely on other people to build our self-image for us and we need to make sure we do it ourselves. One of the easiest ways of doing this is to keep a success file. A success file is simply a folder, a list or a notebook in which you write down all the things that you have achieved and are proud of. We tend to have a natural reluctance to write down our achievements, almost as if we're afraid people will think of us as immodest and big-headed. The success file is for our use only. We don't need to show it to other people, but we do need to refer to it regularly and keep it up to date.

A success file works best when it includes both work related and home related activities. A typical success file may include copies of letters from managers, customers, suppliers or colleagues congratulating us on a job well done. It may include a note to the effect that, on 20 January, someone rang up to say how much they appreciated your work. It may include a note written by your son or daughter saying pleasant things about you, or a card from an old friend saying how much they enjoyed seeing you again. Being successful is being successful in every aspect of your life, not just in one limited area. Success at work, if achieved at the expense of everything else, is a hollow victory. If you include items from work and home in your success file, you will constantly remind yourself of the need for balance.

The next time you have a difficult meeting, an awkward customer, a problem at home or have to do something that is outside of your comfort zone then look through your success file first. We all get self-doubts and we all worry about our ability to succeed. Reminding ourselves of our strengths puts us in a positive frame of mind and increases the probability of achieving yet more successful outcomes.

While some people keep their success file for their eyes only, others like to have reminders of their success on display at the office and in their homes. These reminders may include certificates, trophies, photographs, letters, post-it notes and so on. I used to think that some of these displays of achievement were ostentatious and off-putting and, indeed, they can be if they're displayed in such a way as simply to impress the visitor. Be proud of your achievements but be wary of ostentation.

One of the most effective ways of using a success file in business is to take all the positive, complimentary letters your customers have written about your organisation, put them in a binder and leave them at reception. Zero Mostel, in Mel Brooks's film *The Producers* may have been going slightly too far when he said 'If you've got it, flaunt it', but the basic principle is there. Be proud of your success and continue to remind yourself of what you've achieved.

LIMITS OF PERFORMANCE

We are all capable of the extraordinary, but we also need to be careful that we don't live in a fantasy world where our belief in our abilities exceeds our grasp of reality. There is a fine line between believing we are capable of anything and setting ourselves up to fail. As Figure 15 shows, it is possible for us to make mistakes in either underestimating or overestimating our potential. We all operate with

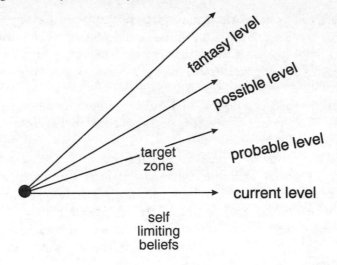

Figure 15: Levels of performance.

a set of self-limiting beliefs that prevent us from achieving our true performance potential. We need to be aware of these limits to our beliefs and expand our horizons so that we can achieve more.

At the other extreme we have to recognise that we cannot achieve the impossible and need to remain aware of our starting point. We may be able to double our income in a year, but few of us are likely to increase it tenfold. This doesn't mean that people shouldn't dream or try for the exceptional. It means that people should be aware of the risks. People do achieve what others think is impossible but most of them have failed at least once along the way and many have paid a high personal price for their success. Be aware of the risks. Managing pressure for peak performance is concerned with raising standards and making conscious, informed decisions about what you want out of life. It is not a mechanism for piling on the pressure in the hope that you will have accumulated as much wealth as possible before you burn out!

Limits are barriers to be broken, but breaking the limits must be based on being able to differentiate between the probable, the possible and the impossible. Go flat out for the probable. If you believe it, it will happen. Try for the possible. If you plan carefully and work at it hard enough, it may happen. Be wary of the impossible. You may be setting yourself up to fail.

HEALTH AND FITNESS

One of the recurring themes throughout this book is the need to maximise our resources in order to deal with pressure effectively. We need to make sure that our minds are able to use the energy of a healthy body to sustain our ability to manage pressure and maximise our available resources. We don't need to be high performing athletes to manage pressure, but we do need to be aware of the need for a healthy mind in a healthy body.

We are designed to be physically active. Spending all day sitting behind a desk or in the seat of a car punctuated by the occasional stroll to the coffee machine is not using our bodies effectively. Our ancestors were highly mobile and would walk twenty to thirty miles a day in pursuit of food. People who get up in the morning, grab a cup of coffee, jump in the car, drive to work, take the lift up to their office and spend most of the day behind their desk, eating a sandwich while they work, then get back in the car, drive home, collapse in front of the television and go to bed, may walk less than a hundred yards during the day. We've seen in Chapter 2 that body chemistry changes in responses to pressure and that the stress reaction produces long-lasting and damaging effects. Exercise helps to dissipate these adverse effects and allows us to return to a more normal state more quickly. We need to be fit and healthy to improve our resourcefulness and to improve our ability to cope with the physical effects of stress.

EXERCISE

Exercise is an excellent way of developing resources. Exercise is not just for the physically fit or the sports enthusiast. It is good for everyone. We get exercise from a huge variety of activities, and don't need to limit ourselves to the gym or fitness centre. Organisations like the Sports Council, the Health Education Authority, local authorities and a wide range of other organisations will provide information about leisure and exercise activities. Exercise should be fun, not a chore, and it is important to choose an activity that you enjoy. There are enough options to choose from that you needn't be forced into doing something that will cause you more pressure and stress. You need to choose a form of exercise that you will stick to and it may be worth sampling a few different activities until you find the one that suits you best.

HEALTHY EATING

We are what we eat. Our bodies are continually renewing themselves as old cells die and are replaced by new ones formed from
the food we eat. We need healthy food to build and maintain a
healthy body. A healthy body provides the energy and resources
we need to manage pressure. It's hard to achieve peak performance
if your body is tired, overweight and continually fed unhealthy
food. You need to think about your eating habits and find a way of
eating that improves your health. There are thousands of different
diets and a host of experts in nutrition all eager to persuade you
that they have found the perfect diet. The advice on healthy eating
is confusing and contradictory, so the only sensible thing to do is to
follow some basic, generally agreed principles and experiment
with different approaches until you find the one that works for
you. The proof of the pudding is literally in the eating.

GOOD HEALTH

Good health means more than an absence of illness. It means
having the energy, vitality, alertness and stamina to manage
pressure and live life to the full. Good health involves understanding
the risk factors responsible for ill health and disease and actively
managing your physical and psychological wellbeing. The subject
of health and fitness is beyond the scope of this book but understanding the issues is a key element in managing pressure. Dr
David Ashton has written an excellent and extremely comprehensive book on health and fitness, *The 12-Week Executive Health Plan*.[3]
This book avoids the jargon and the faddishness of the health and
fitness industry. It is based on sound medical and scientific research
and provides the reader with a carefully devised action programme for evaluating and reducing health risks. If you are
concerned with improving your health I recommend you try this
book.

1   Robbins, A (1989) *Unlimited Power:* Simon & Schuster, New
    York.
2   Robbins, A, op cit.
3   Ashton, David (1993) *The 12-Week Executive Health Plan:*
    Kogan Page, London.

5

Achieving a balance

Roger believes that it is important to keep a balance between home and work. He works hard and is successful, but he works so that he and his family can enjoy a good lifestyle and do the things that they want. A few years ago life wasn't like that. Roger worked long hours, took work home and thought about little else but work. Pamela, his wife, also worked. The two of them had little time to talk to each other, no time to cook and were both preoccupied with their jobs.

Roger's life changed when Pamela became pregnant. The birth of their son had a profound effect on Roger. For the first time in his life he started to think about what he really wanted to do rather than run unthinkingly along the career treadmill. Roger decided that what he really wanted was to be able to spend time with his family, be there as his son grew up and have time to read, go out, take holidays and all the other things that he and Pamela had neglected because they were too busy working.

Roger had a problem. He was currently working long hours under an enormous amount of pressure and only just managing to keep up with what he had to do. How could he possibly make more time for the family without sacrificing his career? He and Pamela had got used to a high standard of living and he was reluctant to give it up. Roger thought about his problem and remembered some of the things he'd been taught but had never learned.

The first thing he remembered was that nobody had ever died saying 'I wish I'd worked harder'. There was more to life than work, and work, instead of being the number one priority, now had to take second place to his family. Roger also remembered that the way to achieve more is to work smarter, not harder. If hard work was the secret of economic success then Third World peasant farmers would be wealthy.

Roger started thinking about his job and the things that really mattered. He realised that he could be better at delegating and needed to improve the office procedures. He also realised how much time he wasted in unproductive meetings or just sitting around after work chatting and drinking coffee. In the past, getting home hadn't been that important, Pamela was working, the house was empty and, he now realised, it was more pleasant to be at work than to be at home.

Now things were different, he wanted to be at home and yet he still wanted to be successful. He realised he may have to make some sacrifices and that, probably the hardest decision of all, he would have to learn to say no.

Roger and Pamela now have two children. Pamela's working part-time so that she can spend some time at home and Roger is still managing to spend a lot of time with his family. He's had another promotion since the birth of his son, and is happier and more relaxed than he ever used to be. Roger and Pamela enjoy their lives. They still work hard but they have far more time to do the other things that really make life worth while. In a way, they've found true success. They've found a balance.

We need balance in our lives: balance between the things we want to do and the things we have to do to get them. We need balance between work and home, and balance between work and play. All work makes Jack a dull boy and leads to a situation in which there is nothing but work. When work stops, life is empty.

RELAXATION AND PERSONAL TIME

Time management

Time is a diminishing resource. We have the time between when we are born and when we die in which to achieve our goals. There is no extra time. Death doesn't get postponed because we are running behind schedule. On any given day we all have the same amount of time available to us, 24 hours, and yet we all use it in very different ways. For some people, there is never enough time, they're constantly rushing, frequently late, always trying to cram more and more things into the day, and would be delighted if they could find a way of getting by on 2 or 3 hours' sleep a night. Other people find that time moves slowly, many of their days are long and boring, and they find themselves watching the clock and waiting until it is time to go to bed.

Why do we view time so differently? Why can some people achieve in an hour what it takes others days to do? The difference isn't just confined to work. It's true in all aspects of our lives, whether it's spending time with our children, cleaning the house, making a meal, writing a report, going to the cinema or whatever. Some of us use time, for others time uses us.

The situation is made more complicated because all of us, as individuals, have some days when we use time efficiently and some days where we fritter it away. We know what it's like to have a really good day when we accomplish everything we set out to do and feel proud of our achievements. At the other extreme we have days that we regard as a complete waste of time, when we might as well have not bothered going into work. We pick things up, put them down and never actually accomplish anything. By the end of the day we have nothing to show for our efforts.

Time Management Systems

The difference between the good and bad days has little to do with the use of a time management system. People with the world's best time management system still have bad days and people who have never used a system have days of incredible efficiency. Yet the huge industry built around time management skills training is based primarily on proprietary 'time management systems'. Almost every training company offers time management courses and there are a large number of organisations who specialise in time management training. Many of these organisations provide their own personal organiser systems and have developed some extremely sophisticated and clever ways of helping people to prioritise and plan their day by identifying key tasks, keeping diaries, managing contact lists and so on.

Time management systems have now extended into computer software where PIMS (personal information managers) are one of the fastest growing product lines. Some of these programmes are wonderful tools for helping to organise your day and get things done. They provide to do lists, address books, diaries and year planners. They include systems for managing contacts, logging calls and automatically dialling numbers. They do almost everything except make the tea. The tools and technologies become increasingly sophisticated and, for many people, myself included, they make a major improvement to productivity. The problem is that no matter how good the personal organiser, or time management system, they cannot manage your time for you. You still have to do it yourself.

Motivation

The issue of time management is not the search for a better system but the need to understand why an individual achieves a lot one day and nothing the next. If you deprive an excellent time manager of their time management system, they would probably still continue to function far more effectively than a poor time manager who has been given the world's best organising system. Time management systems help some people to improve their productivity, but the emphasis on systems misses the point that time management is about motivation not mechanisms. This is the time management trap. The motivation to manage your time is more important than the mechanics of time management. Many people who want to improve their time management skills overlook the need for clearer goals in the search for a better process.

An informal research study we carried out demonstrated this point clearly. We asked people to think about the time when they were most effective and got most done. People felt they were most efficient just before a holiday, when they moved offices or when they changed jobs. Many people come into work on the day before they go on holiday and achieve more in that day than they did in the previous week. They haven't changed their systems, suddenly remembered their time management training or picked a day when they have nothing to do. The difference is one of motivation. They have to clear their desk, tidy up the loose ends and manage their time, so they do it. It's as simple as that. Many people surprise themselves by what they accomplish. They start the day thinking they'll never get everything done and leave with the satisfaction of a clean desk.

The simple answer to improving productivity would therefore appear to be that employers should give everyone a holiday at least once a week. Unfortunately, this is unlikely to be accepted by most bosses and we have to find alternative ways of putting ourselves in the pre-holiday state. One way of doing this is to treat each day as if you would receive a huge reward for achieving the day's objectives. Ask yourself the question, 'What would I accomplish today if I knew I would get £1,000,000 if I'd achieved everything both at home and at work that I should have done?'

Habits

Over time most people develop patterns and ways of working which are inefficient and counter-productive. We know we could improve, but habits are hard to break. If we start the day with a cup of coffee, chat to some people, read the paper, rearrange the papers on our desk, start to make a phone call, pick up another piece of paper, shuffle a few more piles, talk to somebody else and so on, then it's not surprising that we don't start getting things done until the end of the morning. Just as we're getting into our stride, it's time for lunch and, after lunch, the pattern starts all over again and then it is time to go home. We need to break the pattern and find a more efficient way of working. Systems can help but they're not the solution.

Urgent and Important - the key categories

If you need to choose a time management system, make sure it's simple. For many people, the basic principle of being able to differentiate between the urgent and the important is the only system that they need. Most people have problems with time management because they spend their days doing things that are urgent but are not important. The difference is crucial. Things that are urgent are things that have to be done straight away, either because you want to do them or because someone needs them to be done. Things that are important are the things that add value and are jobs on which your performance is judged. Many of these tasks are long term

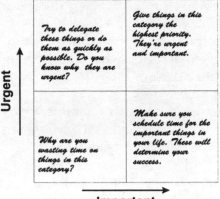

Figure 16: Urgent and important.

projects or activities that require careful preparation and planning. Unfortunately, because they are not urgent, they don't get into the diary or on to the 'to do' list or into the consciousness for that day. Even when these tasks are started, they almost invariably get dropped because 'something more urgent came up'.

Learn to differentiate between the urgent and the important, and manage your time accordingly. Most people have between three and five important tasks that they need to be doing at any one time. These tasks need to be scheduled into the diary and time allocated for their completion.

The things that are urgent can then be examined to see whether they really are urgent and, if so, whether they are also important. This simple classification is the starting point for prioritising the day's work. The above grid shows the relationship between these two elements and how items can be placed on the grid according to their rankings on these two factors.

In deciding how to spend your time, you deal with those things that are urgent and important first, and then allocate the remaining time between long term important projects and short term urgent projects, and ignore those things that are neither urgent nor important. It's unfortunate that people tend to spend the majority of their time on the non-urgent and non-important tasks, and almost none on the important things. You may want to think about an ideal ratio that suits your work and your working style and then spend some time thinking about how you actually spend your time. Time pressure is the difference between how you spend your time and how

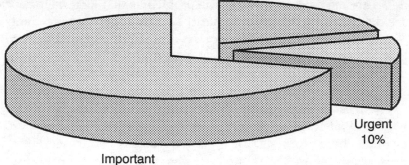

Figure 17: Time Allocation.

you *should* spend your time. Obviously, the amount of time allocated to different types of work will depend on the nature of the job. For example, someone responding to customer service calls is likely to spend a far higher proportion of their time on urgent tasks than an analyst developing a strategic plan. The point is to understand how you actually spend your time compared with how you should spend your time. Figure 17 shows how one manager allocates her time. She spends approximately 30% of her time responding to issues that require her immediate attention. A third of these issues are not particularly important but they are urgent and they have to be done. The manager deals with them quickly and gets them out of the way so they cease to be a source of pressure to her. She is then free to spend most of her time on important, longer term projects. Because she spends 70% of her time on important issues she is highly efficient and is very effective in her job. Think about how you manage your time, and how much time you waste on the trivial or unnecessary. Try to spend the next week improving your time management skills. As an incentive, log the time that you save by working more efficiently and reward yourself by spending half of the saved time on yourself. Leave early, take someone out for lunch, start later or even leave your briefcase at the office instead of taking it home.

Working hours
The time an individual spends at work is not a measure of their effectiveness. In many cases the people who spend longest at their

desks are the most inefficient. The problem is that their inefficiencies are disguised by their hours and they set dangerous precedents in organisations where time at work is more highly valued than what is achieved. The people who use their time inefficiently and make up for it by working long hours create pressure and stress for their subordinates.

The reason people place such a high value on length of time at work is that it's easy to measure. It is far easier for managers to evaluate the performance of staff on the basis of hours worked than it is to measure their effectiveness and their contribution to profitability. This system has a built-in tendency to reward the inefficient and managers should be wary of placing too much emphasis on hours worked.

> Helen is a marketing manager in a computer company. She enjoys her work but doesn't like the long hours. Helen works with six other marketing managers and their assistants. They are all bright, ambitious graduates, eager to further their careers. The problem is that they are all afraid to go home. In Helen's company, working long hours is seen as a sign of commitment and anyone who tries to work a 40-hour week is regarded as a part timer. Helen and her colleagues sit at their desks until 6.30 or 7.30 in the evening waiting for someone to leave so that they don't have to be the first to go home. As Helen says, no one gets much done during this time, but you have to be seen to be there.
>
> Helen's boss is always the last to leave. She thinks she would set a bad example if she left before her staff so she stays to the end. Her husband thinks she spends too long at work and the pressure is beginning to tell. Helen's boss doesn't understand why her marketing managers stay so late; she wishes they would leave a bit earlier so she could go home herself.

Helen's boss has fallen into the trap of thinking that her staff will judge her on the hours she works, not the work she does. It's not only managers that place demands on their staff, it can sometimes be the other way round. In Helen's company they have developed a vicious circle in which everyone spends longer at work than they should. When I discussed the problem with Helen's boss she told me that she would like to change but her director wouldn't understand. She thought I should talk to the board first and get them to go home earlier. I said that change had to start somewhere. Why not with her?

Most of us benefit from working in a structured or semi-structured environment but, in a rapidly changing world, we need to maintain our flexibility. We should be careful, when using systems, not to become a slave to the system. If, by improving time management and delegation skills, you are able to achieve more in less time, then try to resist the temptation of taking on more and more work. Remember the balance between home and work, and reward yourself for your improved time management skills by leaving earlier one night, taking more holiday or not taking work home.

The home – work interface

How we manage our time obviously influences the relationship between home and work. People who are busy at work also tend to have busy home lives. As a consequence they are often under pressure to spend more time at work and to spend more time at home. There are never enough hours in the day to do everything. Inevitably, either work or home, or both, suffer as a result.

The relationship between home and work can be a major source of pressure. Some people find that they ruin their home life because they are too preoccupied with work. Others find that their career suffers because they are not prepared to make the commitment the company expects. Finding the balance is hard.

The home and work relationship is made more complicated because the home, as well as being a source of pressure, can also be an excellent coping mechanism. Talking to a sympathetic and interested partner about the problems at work is a good way to release tension. Hobbies, sports and an active social life can provide a much needed balance for the pressure of work, and can help to maintain a sense of perspective. We need to keep home and work separate, and maintain a balance between the two.

Leaving stress at work

One of the most common problems associated with stress at work is taking worries home with you. People may have a bad day at work, and go home and continue to worry about it. This is bad for the family and tends to ruin the evening as well as the day. The following morning you start your day worrying about the tension at home and you still have the problems from the day before. This can continue day after day, and the cumulative problems make both home and work a misery.

One of the best ways of dealing with this kind of pressure is to compartmentalise your life and leave work problems at work. This is easy to say and hard to do. Most of us are conscientious and worry about things that go wrong at work. However, most of the time we can do nothing about our work problems, and it may be better to go home with a clear mind and forget work until the next day. Some people do this naturally, while others have to learn the skill. The following list suggests a few ways of leaving stress at work.

- As you leave the office, imagine crumpling all the things that have caused you problems during the day up into a ball, and then walking along, tossing the ball over your shoulder and forgetting it. As you throw it away you no longer have the problems to worry about.

- Have an object, a watch for example, that you associate with work. Wear it to work, never anywhere else. When you come home from work take the watch off, put it down and leave the work with the watch. Don't let it interfere with your home life and don't think about work again until you put that watch back on.

- If you wear a business suit or a uniform at work, make sure that it contains the pressures and stresses of the job, and that, when you take it off, you hang up your work. When you come home, no matter how tired you are, it is always a good idea to change from your work clothes to your home clothes.

Similar techniques help people to keep the pressure of the job separate from themselves even when they are at work. Here is an example.

- While you are at work, if you feel under pressure and have problems, simply stand up by the side of your chair and remind yourself that the chair is where the problems are. It is you doing your job who is under pressure. You as an individual are able to get up from that chair, walk away and still be yourself. That brief 30 seconds of standing up next to your chair, looking down at it and seeing that the chair is where the problems lie, can be very beneficial.

As we mentioned at the start of this chapter, we all have the same number of hours in the day. Improving our ability to manage time is probably one of the easiest and most effective mechanisms for managing pressure and enhancing performance. To get more done in less time is an objective we all share and we should take every opportunity to find ways of improving and honing our time management skills.

Relaxation

Relaxation calms the body and the mind, and is probably the most effective way of enabling your body to adjust to its normal level of functioning when you are under stress. It also allows the subconscious to work more effectively in resolving problems. Relaxing is easy and natural when we are on holiday or sitting quietly, away from the pressures of work. Relaxing is hard and difficult to achieve when we are at work, under pressure and need it most. It isn't helpful to be told to relax when you're tense, suffering from stress, annoyed or irritable. In many cases, being told to relax or take it easy has the opposite effect to the one intended, and just adds another frustration to a long list of annoyances. We need the skill to recognise when we should relax and the ability to relax when we want to. To achieve this objective we cannot take relaxation for granted and need to practise relaxation techniques.

You can learn a wide range of relaxation methods from books or tapes, or by going to classes. Some forms of relaxation have spiritual connotations and the techniques of meditation are very similar to those of relaxation. Some people find that religious ceremonies are an excellent way to relax.

One of the simplest ways to relax is to relax the body progressively, starting with the toes and slowly working up the body, relaxing every muscle in turn. Don't worry about letting your mind relax or go blank. You are bound to get stray thoughts flitting across your consciousness. If you practise the technique and do it in the right surroundings you will soon find that mental calmness comes with physical relaxation. It is also useful to learn techniques for quick relaxation and exercises you can do in the office. Relaxation is a powerful tool in managing pressure and it is well worth practising relaxation techniques until you find one that suits your own particular style.

Breathing

The ability to control our breathing is an extremely powerful tool in managing pressure. Even if you haven't time to relax you should try to find time for breathing exercises. All you need to do to start the calming process is to be conscious of your breathing, slow it down and breathe more deeply. Nervousness, panic and stress are all associated with shallow, quick breathing. The next time you're under pressure, just pause for a moment and become conscious of your breathing. Remember what it feels like when you are under stress. When someone around you is panicking or really upset, observe the way they breathe. In contrast, the next time you are feeling totally relaxed, perhaps in a warm bath or sitting in the sunshine, take a moment to become conscious of your breathing, and try and recognise the difference between this and breathing under stress. The two forms are very different and, as we have already seen, we can change the way we feel by changing our physiology. When we breathe in a calm relaxed manner, we become calm and relaxed. Controlling our breathing is another link in the chain that forces our mind into a calmer frame.

The great thing about managing your breathing is that you can do it anywhere. You can do it in the office, in a car, even in a meeting, and the more you practise the techniques the easier it will become to put yourself into a calmer state of mind. Remember, the body tells the brain how to feel. If your body is relaxed and calm, and breathing quietly, slowly and deeply, sooner or later your mind will follow suit. The next time you go into a sales presentation, start a difficult discussion with your boss, talk to suppliers or have a discussion with your children about tidying up their room, try the breathing exercises beforehand and notice how it calms you down.

Starting the day more slowly

An excellent way of active relaxation is to start the day more slowly. Many of us start our days by dragging ourselves wearily from our beds, and hurrying to get ready before running out of the house and rushing to work. The day begins with frantic activity, trying to do all the things we have to do for ourselves, and sometimes the family, and still make sure we get to work on time. For those of us who have to get the children ready for school in the morning, this period can be even more stressful and, by the time we've struggled through the traffic, we arrive at work feeling tired and exhausted.

If this scene is familiar, then it may be helpful for you to start your day more slowly by either reorganising some of your activities so they can be done the night before, or getting up an hour earlier. This may be difficult at first and, like many of these stress tips, don't feel you have to do it every day. Occasionally, perhaps once a week to start with, make a conscious decision to get up and enjoy the morning. Go for a walk, have a bath, read the newspaper, eat a leisurely breakfast. Do something you enjoy that gives you time for yourself before the morning rush begins.

Making time for yourself

As well as starting your day more slowly, try to make time for yourself. One of the problems of family life is that it is often difficult to find time to be by yourself. If you have children, they can make demands on you almost continually. Work and social life also take up a lot of time, and people can go for long periods without really ever having time by themselves to do the things that they want to do. Time to think, time to relax and time to be just by yourself are very important, and you should try and find a way of creating these opportunities.

The major reason people don't take enough time for themselves is the feeling of guilt. We feel guilty if we're not working, even more guilty if we indulge ourselves by sitting down, reading a magazine and having a cup of tea instead of cleaning the house. But why not try it? Do you really have to do a particular household chore today? Why not treat yourself? Instead of rushing straight home or spending your lunch hour shopping, why not buy a magazine - go for a walk in the park, go to a cafe or do whatever makes you feel good. The better you feel, the more able you will be to do the household jobs when you choose to do them.

MAKE TIME FOR YOURSELF TO BE YOURSELF

Figure 18: Make time for yourself to be yourself.

6

Communication Skills

Claire was a middle manager in a highly results-oriented organisation who had recently been promoted into a marketing role. She had moved to head office and was eager to make a good impression. One Friday afternoon, the deputy chairman rang and asked her if she knew how much imported raw material was used in her products. Claire didn't know and was embarrassed at not knowing. However, she said she would find out by Monday morning. Claire asked around in the department but nobody else seemed to know the figure or where to find it. So, eager to please, she worked all weekend analysing the origins of the raw materials supplies to find the proportions for each product line. She persuaded her secretary to come in on Sunday to type up the report and by 9.00 on Monday morning walked proudly into the deputy chairman's office with a 30-page report, complete with graphs and tables showing the percentages of imported materials by product range. The chairman looked at the report and asked her what it was. Claire explained that it was the analysis of raw materials he had asked about on Friday. 'You needn't have gone to that trouble', said the chairman. 'I only wanted to know because my son was doing something on the balance of trade for his economics homework'.

The story is about a failure in communication, but it's also about the danger of false assumptions. The marketing manager assumed that because the deputy chairman was calling her with a request for some specific information, it must be important. At the very least, it was needed for a presentation to the board, a speech he would be giving to the Confederation of British Industry or some other major event. To the chairman it was an inconsequential query, a chance question it would be interesting to have a rough idea about. It never occurred to him that someone would think the question was so important they would work all weekend to find the answer. It never occurred to Claire that the deputy chairman would ring her personally with a request for trivial information.

COMMUNICATING WITH OTHERS

Making assumptions

We need to make assumptions to make sense of the world. Business would stop if every time someone was asked to do something they checked all the assumptions behind the request. Assumptions provide a shorthand way of getting things done quickly. Most of the time, our assumptions serve us well and allow us to get things done. However, we can be mistaken. When we feel we are being put under pressure, it's worth checking to see whether we have correctly understood what we're being asked to do.

Phrases such as 'What exactly do you mean by...?', 'When precisely do you want that?', 'How much time do you want me to spend on this?', 'Do you want a one-page summary or a full report?', 'How much do you want to spend on this?' all help to clarify the task. Anything we are asked to do can be defined in terms of quantity, quality, cost and time. These four factors can be used to eliminate uncertainty. In the above example, if Claire had asked, 'How much detail would you like me go into?', 'How much time should I spend on this?', 'How accurate do you want the data to be?' and 'When do you need it by?', she would have saved herself an enormous amount of work.

Clear communication is particularly important for those of us who have managerial roles. We tend to make a lot of assumptions about the amount of knowledge that people have and the way they think about situations. The problem with challenging assumptions is that we would get very little done and communication would be so stilted as to be unworkable if we questioned every task in detail. The key to success in clarifying ambiguous tasks is to use your judgement. Ask what you need to ask. The world is full of people doing unnecessary work because assumptions have not been challenged and the task has not been clearly defined.

Understanding the job

At work, improving communication skills is only part of the solution. Employees will continue to make false assumptions if they are confused about the purpose of their job. They have to understand their role so thoroughly that they don't need to be told what to do. They should understand the context and know what is required without the need for detailed explanation. This approach deals with the problem at source. If people understand their role in contributing to the business, they don't need to worry about confusing messages. People are far more effective if they focus on the contribution they can make to the organisation rather than their tasks. Anything that limits an individual's ability to contribute to the success of the organisation is a potential source of pressure and a potential area for communication breakdown. This is why job descriptions and key tasks can be so damaging. In the days of industrial disputes, one of the worst things a union could threaten was a 'work to rule'. Working to rule, doing exactly what the agreements say, is a recipe for disaster, and both management and unions knew it. Attempts to break jobs down into their component parts are doomed to failure. Organisations should emphasise the individual's role and the contribution they can make to the goals of the organisation, not the task.

Sharing the vision

There is a world of difference in attitude when organisations manage to communicate the vision clearly. There is an old story about a man going into a quarry and seeing three stonemasons at work. He asked each of them in turn what they were doing. The first stone-mason said he was cutting stone. The second stone mason said he was making stone blocks, and the third stone mason smiled and stood proudly by his piece of stone. 'I am helping to build a cathedral,' he said. The three men are all doing the same job, working in the same conditions, but the first knows his task, the second knows his job and the third understands his contribution. Which of these would you like to have in your organisation?

Listening skills

Clear communication is essential for managing pressure and achieving peak performance. The ability to communicate is a skill that can be developed and, for most of us, the most important skill is the ability to listen. There is a world of difference between listening actively to what people say and hearing the words that they speak. Listening is about understanding and about receiving the message. Listening involves the use of a wide range of techniques to make sure that we understand clearly what the other person is trying to say. This may involve clarifying, checking, confirming and restating so that the other person understands that the message has been received correctly.

We can learn a lesson about the importance of checking for understanding from the computer industry. Transferring data between computers has to be accurate and computer engineers have evolved a set of protocols to enable computers to talk to each other. These protocols provide efficient mechanisms for ensuring that the message received is the same as the message that is sent. The computer will not carry on sending data unless it knows that the previous part has been received correctly.

In human communication we have no formal mechanism for error checking and conversations often proceed by building misunderstanding upon misunderstanding. We have seen from our research that poor communications are one of the biggest causes of pressure. People frequently say, 'Nobody understands me', 'My boss doesn't understand me', 'My partner doesn't understand me'. We feel frustrated, angry and misunderstood because we are unable to communicate clearly with the people around us. Although there are many occasions when communication is difficult and ineffective, there are also times when we can communicate an enormous amount of information with a glance, a gesture or a couple of words. The difference in these two states, the failure to communicate despite using thousands of words and the ability to communicate by raising an eyelid, are explained by differences in empathy and sensitivity.

In a work situation, one of the most difficult skills for a manager or supervisor to learn is how to listen to your staff. Listening to the people who work for you is difficult because there are barriers on both sides. People don't expect bosses to listen to what they have to say. Their expectation of the world of work is that they will be told what to do and any attempts to discuss the issue may be seen as insubordination. Fortunately, this attitude is changing and an increasing number of organisations are taking a much more active role in encouraging their employees to talk to their managers. This is discussed in more detail in Chapter 8 in the section on employee participation. Managers should be approachable and make sure they create opportunities for their employees to talk to them about issues which matter.

Saying it now

We all know about the little, niggling irritations that, because nothing was said, build up until they make us really angry. Living with someone with an annoying habit, like leaving the top off the toothpaste, cutting their toenails in bed or not rinsing the bath out after they've finished, may start out as a minor irritation and, over time, build up to serious resentment. It's the same at work. We may be under pressure because a colleague continually does something that annoys us. She may not even be aware of it and probably has no idea of how irritating it is. Because she doesn't think it annoys people she will carry on doing it for the future. In these cases the sooner we say something, the better it is and the calmer we can be during the discussion. Instead of wasting months building up resentment, anger and irritation that could all come out in a torrent of abuse when we finally have a confrontation, we simply deal with the situation when it arises in a friendly, constructive and positive way.

In these situations humour is a wonderful asset. It is possible to deal with highly sensitive issues if they're done with humour and kindness. Using humour to make a point helps to finish the matter quickly without any bad feeling. The important thing to remember about humour in this context is that it mustn't be directed against the other person. Making someone the victim of a joke is not a sympathetic way of communicating with them.

Congruence

The other important element is that of intent. What do you mean by what you are trying to say? Communication is most effective when the message is congruent with the meaning. People are surprisingly good at picking up hidden messages and the truth behind the words. We should be wary of saying things because we think we ought to say them. If we have to discuss a difficult subject with someone, perhaps a disciplinary matter, then we should think about our feelings on the subject and, ideally, work on them until they are consistent with what we are trying to say. We may, for example, be put into the position where we have to fire someone or make them redundant. It's very hard to be positive in these circumstances, but we can do it sensitively. Being made redundant is bad enough, but being told you've lost your job by somebody who obviously doesn't care less is even more distressing. What's even worse is being told you've lost your job by somebody who obviously doesn't care but is trying to pretend to be sympathetic and understanding.

John was made redundant from a chemical company after almost 25 years' service. He had joined the business as an apprentice and was proud of having worked his way up into a responsible, supervisory role. He prided himself on his loyalty to the firm, the quality of his work and his excellent attendance record. He knew the business was in trouble and, with a number of his friends having already lost their jobs, wasn't surprised when his firm announced they were making a further 100 people redundant.

The redundancy notice wasn't handled particularly well, but what made John furious was being summoned to the personnel officer's office and being told he was on the redundancy list. At John's age, he had expected that he might be on the list and had prepared himself for the shock of redundancy. He hadn't prepared himself to be told he was leaving the company by someone half his age, whom he had hardly seen and who kept getting his name wrong while delivering meaningless platitudes about John's first rate contribution to the firm. Like most people, John wanted to be treated with respect and dignity. If bad news has to be given, it should be communicated honestly and with integrity.

It's probably true to say that more pressure and stress are caused by failures in communication than any other factor. Many organisations are extremely poor at communicating with their employees and sometimes there is a complete failure of senior management to understand the way that their staff feel about the company. We need to think more clearly about how we communicate with people and we need to be more sensitive to feedback.

SOCIAL SUPPORT

One of the most common ways of coping with pressure is through talking to people. 'A burden shared is a burden halved'.

> 'I find myself getting really worked up sometimes. Things seem to be going wrong and I get right to the end of my tether. Sometimes it gets so bad I feel I'm going to scream, but I find that when I sit down at coffee and have a good talk about my problems, then, after I've got it off my chest, I can just get back to work and everything's OK again'.

One of the worst things that we can do with pressure is 'bottle it up'. It's like trying to keep the lid tightly down on boiling water. Eventually the pressure builds up to such an extent that it has to find a way out. In the worst case, the pot explodes with disastrous consequences. It is the same for people. The higher the pressure and the more it's repressed, the worse the consequences when things break down. Talking to people about your problems is an excellent way of reducing the build-up of pressure.

Most of our problems don't seem quite so big when we've had a chance to talk about them and if there's someone around the table who can make a joke about the situation and get people laughing, then that's even better. Talking about pressure with supervisors and managers, although harder to do, can also be very beneficial. Often pressure is caused by people thinking that their managers or supervisors don't understand what's going on and don't realise how much work is involved in doing what you've been asked to do. You may have to choose your time and place carefully, and you may even need to plan what you're going to say beforehand, but if you're able to explain your feelings to your boss about something that's troubling you, then you can clear the air and get on with your job with a more positive attitude. Quite often, the boss won't be able to do anything about what's caused the problem, but the fact that they know, and have listened and understood, makes everyone feel better.

If you have people working for you, try to think about how you can improve your listening skills and try to create opportunities that allow people to talk to you about issues that matter to them. We're not suggesting that you encourage 'moan sessions' or try and take on the role of a counsellor, but simply think about the amount of time you really spend listening to your staff and how approachable you are. There are very few people whose problems are not reduced by being able to talk about them.

COMMUNICATION TECHNIQUES

There are many approaches to understanding and improving the techniques of communication. Two that I have found most useful in managing pressure are Transactional Analysis (TA) and Neuro Linguistic Programming (NLP). TA and NLP provide an excellent framework for understanding the process of communication, and you may benefit from further reading in these subjects if the brief descriptions in this book seem relevant.

Transactional Analysis

Transactional Analysis is the method of examining the communication between people. It was developed by a psychiatrist, Dr Eric Berne, who isolated and defined the basic unit of communication. He described it as follows:

> The unit of social intercourse is called a transaction. If two or more people encounter each other ... sooner or later one of them will speak, or give some other indication of acknowledging the presence of others. This is called the transactional stimulus. Another person will then say or do something which is in some way related to the stimulus and that is called the transactional response.[1]

Eric Berne and other writers on TA have produced an elaborate and complex set of models to describe transactions. Although we can't tackle the subject thoroughly in this book, it is worth thinking about some of the basic principles in more detail. It's not necessary to understand the theory in any depth to use the principles of TA to help improve your communication skills. Simply thinking about why communications with certain people may not work as well as they should in terms of the number of transactions, the nature of the transactions and the games that people are playing will help you to understand how to take the appropriate action to improve the way you communicate.

The theory of TA has been developed on the basis that from the time of our birth we all need to be stimulated. Infants who have been deprived of physical contact over a long time will tend to 'sink into an irreversible decline' and are more likely to succumb to disease. These illnesses can be fatal and research has shown that we need stimulus to survive. The most effective form of stimulation is physical stimulation. With babies, this stimulation can be described as stroking. Stroking doesn't literally mean stroking, but can mean hugging, patting, kissing or whatever. Berne describes a stroke as a fundamental unit of social action and an exchange of strokes is a transaction.

We all need stroking and, as we would expect, some people need a larger number of strokes and a greater variety of strokes than others. In our society, once we grow out of being babies the stroking becomes social rather than physical. We receive strokes from other people as a result of the things that they say or the way they look at us or the letters they write. We get under pressure and feel threatened when we fail to get the number of strokes we need.

Playing games

In *The Games People Play,* Berne described a game as 'An ongoing series of complementary ulterior transactions progressing to a well-defined, predictable outcome'.[2] Berne describes a whole series of games under the broad headings of Life Games, Marital Games, Party Games, Sexual Games and so on. Berne describes a typical game as an 'If it weren't for you'. The basis of the 'If it weren't for you' game is that it allows one of the partners to avoid doing all the things that they are afraid of by blaming it on the more dominant partner. 'If it weren't for you, I could have had a successful career. If it weren't for you I could have been a really good dancer' and so on.

Berne gives an example of a group of women who meet regularly for coffee and play 'If it weren't for him', where the conversation revolves around the telling of 'If it weren't for him' stories. Berne described the importance of this game playing in the way that a newcomer to the coffee morning group would be invited to play 'If it weren't for him'. If she plays the game well then she will quickly become a close member of the social circle. If she insists on taking a more charitable view of her husband and refuses to play the game, then she will soon be ostracised.

It's easy to see the same games being played at work. In any organisation there's usually at least one 'moan table' where people can go in their lunch hour and play 'If it weren't for the ...'. These games are almost always destructive and revolve around all the wonderful things that the participants could have done if it weren't for their boss, their staff, customers, suppliers or whoever. People can spend most of their working lives playing 'If it weren't for ...', and seem to need a regular opportunity to complain and moan about work. Because this game is so common, people play it to be accepted by the group without really meaning it. Like the woman going to the coffee mornings in Berne's example, if she wants to have friends in the new neighbourhood she needs to play their games.

At work, the people who are the most frequent players of 'If it weren't for ...' may be some of the strongest and most forceful characters in the company. The moan sessions are usually destructive and, because of the strength of the characters playing the game, a negative, critical attitude becomes accepted as the norm. Fortunately, we find that many people stop playing the game instantly when they understand what is going on. Instead of spending their lunch hours moaning, they get out of the building and take a proper break or they make it a rule not to play that game at their table. They find that their attitude towards their employer starts to change and that they find themselves able to go back to work in a more positive frame of mind.

Neuro Linguistic Programming

Neuro Linguistic Programming (NLP) is a recent development in applied psychology and is the 'art and science of personal excellence'.[3] NLP provides a powerful range of tools and techniques for personal development. It is used in counselling, education and business and includes many techniques that help in managing pressure. NLP was developed in the 1970s by John

Grinder, a professor of linguistics and Richard Bandler, a psychology student, both at the University of Santa Cruz, California. Bandler and Grinder studied three top therapists and, by analysing the underlying patterns in their widely different styles, produced models of successful therapy. Bandler and Grinder used these patterns to develop a model of effective communication and personal change. They called their approach Neuro Linguistic Programming. Since then NLP has developed into the study of patterns of excellence and effective ways of thinking and communication.

NLP, as well as being an excellent set of techniques for personal change, is also a very powerful tool for improving interpersonal communications. In communication, we confuse quantity with quality. If we have problems communicating with someone, we don't necessarily need to use more words. We simply need to use the right words. The right words are the ones that will be understood by the listener, who will use their language, their frame of reference and their way of looking at the world to make sense of what we say. This is obvious when we think about London businesspeople communicating with someone from an Amazonian tribe, but it is harder to appreciate when the two people work in the same office. However, the barriers may still be there. If we fail to understand the other person's perspective then our communications with them will always be difficult.

One approach to understanding how we communicate, and how we can improve our communication skills, is a set of techniques for mirroring and matching other people. Some people, the good communicators, do this automatically. They 'wear a face to meet the faces that they meet'. In a way they are a little like chameleons, in that they may subtly change their accent, their stance, their vocabulary and possibly even their views, depending on whom they're talking to. They may do it completely unconsciously but are able to make friends with, and feel at home with, almost everyone they meet.

The rest of us need to understand more about the techniques so that we can improve our own communication abilities. The first of these techniques is understanding that not everyone interprets the world in the same way. Some people are highly visual; they make sense of the world primarily through what they see. Others are auditory; they interpret the world through what they hear. Other people are kinaesthetic; they act on the basis of their feelings or emotions. Communication can be difficult when a visual person is having a discussion with an auditory or kinaesthetic person. Visual people tend to speak quickly; they try to make their words keep pace with the images in their mind. Auditory people choose their words carefully and therefore speak more slowly. Kinaesthetic people speak more slowly still. They react to their feelings and their words reflect the way they feel about the subject. The language as well as the pace is also different. Visual people will use visual metaphors; 'It looks like ... ', 'I see what you mean.'. Auditory people say 'Sounds OK to me ...', 'I hear what you're saying...'. Kinaesthetic people use physical phrases; 'It feels good to me', 'I'll go along with that'. When we talk to someone we rarely think about the way that they interpret our conversation and miss the clues that indicate the discussion is going wrong because of the differences in representation. Pressure can come from conversations where the people involved all want the same result but fail to realise it because of their different styles.

Sensitivity

Improving communication skills is not about improving your ability to manipulate people. It is concerned with breaking down the barriers between people so that we get on better together or work together more effectively. As we have seen, the art of good communication is sensitivity to the needs of others. Being able to see the world through other people's eyes, ears or feelings is a very valuable, and very rare, skill. Most of the time we are so engrossed with our own lives, and our needs and desires, that we simply fail to take into account other people's needs.

Ironically, some of the people for whom we cause the most problems are the ones closest to us. Our family and friends, and the people who work for us, tend to be the ones whom we take most for granted and are the ones with whom we make the least effort to communicate. Because we know people, we think we understand them and we also think we have no need to try. If we are going to change the way that we communicate with other people, we should start with those who are closest to us. We need to remind ourselves of a few key questions.

• Did they understand what I was trying to say?

- Do they understand why I was trying to say it?
- How can I tell if they have understood?

Sensitivity to the needs of others, combined with the use of TA and NLP techniques, will reduce the pressure from poor communications and improve your ability to share your feelings with other people. In this way improving communications provides a double benefit. It enables you to deal with pressure at its source and it also enhances your coping skills. Improving communication is probably the single most important technique for reducing pressure. For some people, better communication will remove all their major sources of pressure.

Touching

Touching is taboo in our western society, yet it is also an extremely powerful and effective way of communicating with people. There is no better way of showing our regard and feelings for someone than to pat them on the back, or give them a hug or just shake their hand and say well done. This touching can be misused, particularly if it is between members of the opposite sex, and can be seen as a come on, insulting or as sexual harassment.

The important thing to remember about touching is that it should be real, and a genuine demonstration of affection and warmth towards someone else for a job well done, and should not be forced or put on. The touch should come from the heart and the critical element is that you should touch without taking. In other words you are giving someone a pat on the back because you want to give them something, not because you want something from them.

Remember the phrase, 'touch without taking'; it will help to make sure that you are expressing genuine feelings to which the other person can respond and agree to accept.

References

[1]   Berne, E (1964) *The Games People Play:* Grove Press, New York.
[2]   Berne, E, op cit.

7

Managing Mood

Derek is always complaining. Nothing ever seems to go right for him and, whatever happens, it is always a problem. If Derek won a million pounds on the pools he would be upset because he could have won an extra five thousand if Bristol Rovers had managed to scrape a draw. Derek is a born pessimist. Everything he does goes wrong and for some unknown reason he never seems to be as lucky as other people. He thinks he was born unlucky. I think he made himself this way.

Derek works as an accountant in a large manufacturing company. He's very bright and, technically, very good at his job. Of course, he works more hours than anyone else in the company and, although he has a reasonably senior role, younger people who don't know half of what he knows are promoted ahead of him. Derek now realises that his career is going nowhere. Because he works such long hours he doesn't have much of a home life. He doesn't seem to have many friends and his wife, although very long suffering, doesn't seem to be particularly happy.

Derek blames his circumstances. If the kids hadn't had problems with their schooling, he could have moved to a better job a few years ago. If his wife didn't want to live near her family, they could have moved to a better house on the other side of town. Derek doesn't seem to have many friends at work although he's been there for 20 years. People are polite to him, they ask him how he's getting on, but nobody ever seems to spend much time with him. He tends to have a sandwich at his desk while he works, but occasionally he'll come to the canteen and have a hot meal. He sat by himself yesterday. No one joined him.

INTERNAL COMMUNICATIONS

As well as improving the way we communicate with other people we should also improve the way we communicate with ourselves. We act according to our beliefs about ourselves and we establish ways of thinking that shape our behaviours. If we have strong negative beliefs and a low self-image we constantly communicate messages of inadequacy to ourselves and produce poor results. We set ourselves up to fail. Some people achieve a certain satisfaction from being able to tell themselves, 'Well, I knew I couldn't do that'. We are capable of making ourselves fail in our jobs, in our marriages, in our relationships with our children and in all aspects of our life.

For many people, failure is so ingrained that they may go through their whole lives being miserable and depressed, without ever realising that they are the source of their own downfall. To achieve peak performance and manage pressure effectively, we need to change our belief systems to positive, success oriented beliefs. There is a well-known phrase about beliefs, 'If you think you can or if you think you can't, you're right'. We need to teach ourselves to think that we can, to understand the art of the possible and to make sure we get the outcomes that we want.

POSITIVE SELF-IMAGE

The best way to get other people to like you is to like yourself. If you don't feel good about yourself, nobody else will. Positive thinking is a way of raising your self-esteem. It changes your perceptions of yourself and leads to changes in behaviour. Positive thinking underlies many of the principles discussed in this book, and it has obvious links to the way in which we perceive threats and the resources we use to cope with pressure. We have already seen that the more capable and competent we are, the more able we are to deal with pressure and the less we perceive situations as threatening. Enhancing self-esteem, taking a positive view of a situation and turning problems into opportunities are all aspects of positive thinking.

MANAGING FEELINGS

The way we feel, the way we behave and way we react to pressure are all linked to our physiology. When we are tired, run down, ill, suffering from a hangover or overeating, then our bodies will not be in a resourceful state and our ability to manage pressure is diminished. We don't need to be experts in physical fitness to understand that the fitter and healthier our bodies, the more energy and resources will be available to deal with pressure and the less vulnerable we will be.

The relationship between the mind and the body is an interesting one and, in order to manage pressure effectively, we need to understand how to use our mind to control our body and use our body to control our feelings. Pressure comes from perceiving an event as a threat. Our minds decide how we are going to represent that threat to ourselves and we act accordingly.

The body teaches the mind how to feel. We know from our own experience and by observing others that if we are in a depressed state, feeling fed up and run down, our bodies adopt a certain posture. We put our heads down, look to the ground, droop our shoulders, curve our back, take shallow breaths and look sad. Take a moment to feel this for yourself. Stop reading and adopt a depressed posture. If you stay in this position for more than a few seconds, you will automatically start feeling less resourceful, less powerful and less positive that you were when you started. Now stand up straight, put your head back, lift your eyes up, put your chest out, breath deeply and smile. You will instantly feel better. It is that easy to change the way we feel. We do not have to accept feeling fed up or depressed. We can decide that we want to be cheerful and create this state simply by changing our physiology.

Just watch people around you. You can tell the powerful, resourceful people by the way they look, stand and walk. The phrase 'Grin and bear it' is sound advice. If you get into a difficult situation then the first thing you must do is change your physiology so that you are in a powerful state. When you're faced with a threat you need to marshal all your resources. You don't want to limit yourself by trying to act in a depressed, weak and vulnerable state. Grinning or smiling in the face of adversity is a quick and easy way of enhancing your ability to deal with the problem.

Chapter 4 showed the importance of a positive self image. You can combine positive thinking with a resourceful physiology by talking to yourself as you alter your state. If you drive to work in the morning try looking at yourself in the mirror, putting a huge grin on your face and saying loudly and positively 'I feel great'. You may feel embarrassed the first few times you do this but persevere. Doing this just before you start work means that you will start your day with increased energy and resources and are capable of tackling anything. Before going into an important meeting, look in the mirror and give yourself a big grin. Stand tall, smile, breathe regularly and you will walk into the meeting in a positive, powerful state ready to handle anything.

By changing your physiology in this way you not only influence the way that you feel about yourself but you also influence the way that other people feel about you. Think about how you would react to someone who comes to see you and walks in with their head down, avoids eye contact and looks as if they wish that the floor would open up and swallow them. No matter what that person has to say, however good or well thought out their contribution, you are predisposed to receive their messages negatively. The person who walks into a room positively, confidently and dynamically, who makes eye contact with the people around and seems controlled and calm will automatically have us on their side. Unless, of course, they go too far and become arrogant and pushy.

There is a fine line between getting it right and going over the top. You should feel good about yourself and let your natural confidence in your abilities come across to other people but shouldn't be arrogant. Be sensitive to the behaviour of others and match your pace with theirs. The most overbearing and arrogant individuals are usually shy and insecure people who overcompensate for their weakness and alienate others in the process.

Just as changing our physiology changes the way we feel, the way we feel changes our physiology. We can use this knowledge to increase self awareness and actively manage the way we think and feel. If we don't like the way we feel we can do something about it. We don't have to passively accept frustration or depression. When something goes wrong or we get under pressure, our bodies change as a result of the stress reaction. As we have seen, the initial response is positive. We become energised and think more clearly. As time goes on we exhaust our adaptation energy and, unless we consciously intervene to change our physiology, we may find ourselves drifting into a dulled, less resourceful, state. We need to recognise when this happens and consciously switch back into a positive state. This is easier to say than to do but it is a very powerful technique for handling pressure. You are controlling your response and extending your boundaries.

The next time you are depressed, worried or under stress, go into the 'Go Positive' stance. Change the way you stand, the way you breathe and the way you smile. Instead of letting your body drift into a stress state simply say to yourself 'Go Positive' and change. We need triggers and reminders to help us access these positive states and it's worth practising your most resourceful stance so that you can go into a positive state whenever you need to.

Anchoring

Changing states, putting yourself into a more resourceful frame of mind, is an important element in the field of Neuro Linguistic Programming. The technique for instantly changing states, as taught by the NLP practitioners, is called anchoring. Anchoring, as the name suggests, is the process by which an action or phrase is linked to and triggers a particular state. Anchors occur naturally or they can be learnt. Music is a good natural anchor. A particular song can have such powerful associations that just hearing a few bars will change your state. The song triggers good or bad memories and you find yourself happier or sadder accordingly. To put yourself into a resourceful state combine an action with the desired state. Pick a phrase or a word, click your fingers or touch your arm or some other part of your body when you go into these positive states, and establish a relationship between the phrase or the action and the positive state. Doing this regularly will enable you to trigger the positive state instantly without other people being aware of what is going on.

Modelling success

One of the most effective ways of achieving what we want and improving our internal communications is through a process of modelling. Modelling is something that we all do some of the time, but we do it subconsciously and in a haphazard way. As children we learn to walk, talk and communicate by modelling the behaviour of adults. As we grow up, we tend to copy or model ourselves on people whom we admire. We emulate some of the phrases that they use, and certain tones of voice and language. Think about some of the phrases and the language that your children use; the phrasing and intonation may be a perfect imitation of a parent or older child.

My consultancy work enables me to spend time with a number of very successful people who are leaders in their field. They have achieved success by being able to manage pressure effectively and they make use of a wide range of coping skills. Most of them respond to high pressure by concentrating their energies and activities on the task in hand. Their focus becomes razor sharp. They act quickly and decisively, while maintaining their balance and sense of perspective by using humour.

They don't panic and, although they all admit being under pressure, few of them show any outward signs of stress. Their attitude is that something has happened, something has gone wrong, and they need to deal with it and make it right again. They don't waste time by being angry or frustrated or worrying about 'Why has this happened to me?' They just concentrate on the job in hand and deal with the issue in a logical, calm, considered way. They are confident of the outcomes, and take action and make decisions that are consistent with those outcomes. There is little, if any, wasted effort.

The role of modelling in managing pressure is to model excellence. It is deliberately to seek out and model those characteristics that enable people to deal with pressure successfully. Many of us feel uncomfortable with copying, as we are taught from a very early age that copying is wrong and that we should do things on our own. However, life is far too short to reinvent the wheel and we should learn what we can from the successful behaviours of the people around us. We should decide which elements of those behaviours produce excellent results and see if we can apply that to our own behaviour. We need to do this carefully and be sure that the behaviours we model are the ones that produce the outcomes we want. Junior managers often make mistakes when they model themselves on senior managers. They copy some of the extreme, perhaps idiosyncratic, behaviours and miss the other, more subtle, behaviours that achieve the results.

This inappropriate modelling can be seen in some of our larger companies. One large manufacturing company recruited graduates into the business and, as part of their training programme, seconded them as assistants to successful senior managers. One of these managers was a forceful, somewhat abrasive individual who nevertheless got excellent results. The graduate trainees and junior managers subconsciously copied his style, believing that being brash, abrasive and sometimes rude was the way to get on in the business. They failed to emulate the success of the senior manager because they only modelled the obvious behaviours. The senior manager was successful in spite of his abrasive style, not because of it. His success was due to his enthusiasm for the business, his willingness to listen and the respect he had for his staff. The people who worked for him tolerated his rudeness because they knew from experience that he was accessible, fair and consistent. Unfortunately, the trainees failed to notice that side of his personality, and couldn't understand why people thought they were rude and uncaring while the senior manager, who was notorious for his rudeness, was well liked and well respected.

So make sure that you model the excellent behaviours, not the smoke-screen that surrounds them. One way of doing this is to try and identify people who are successful 'in their own way', and find out what it is that they have in common. Find out why, for example, two or three managers in a company seem able to manage pressure effectively. Then find two or three other managers who suffer so much from stress that they always seem to be at breaking point, and try to analyse the differences between the successful and the unsuccessful managers. The clues may be hard to find but they will be there. There are reasons why people are successful and success leaves clues. Observing how other people respond when under extreme pressure provides an excellent opportunity for helping to manage pressure in ourselves. Often in these circumstances the superficial behaviours are stripped away and we are left with the core behaviours that allow someone to overcome pressure.

Authenticity

In my work with senior directors and managers of large organisations, I am constantly surprised by how many people feel unable to be themselves at work. It's as if they put on a mask when they put on their work clothes and spend their working days pretending to be somebody else. There are topics they can't talk about, and they often have to disguise their values and beliefs. Many people pretend to be tougher, less feeling and more aggressive than they really are, because they think that these are the behaviours that their company expects. If they act sympathetically or show their feelings, or admit they have a social conscience, then they fear being different from their colleagues. This feeling can be very widespread. In one organisation that is renowned for its tough, aggressive approach, the majority of the senior management team had radically different beliefs to those they expressed in public. They fell into the common communication trap of making assumptions about the way other people felt without ever speaking to them about it.

Not being authentic is a major source of pressure. It's very hard to act naturally if you have to guess the way people would respond to a certain set of circumstances. Good management relies a lot on intuition, flair and backing your judgement. To do this effectively you need to be 'in tune' with yourself and feel able to trust your feelings. If your working day is spent pretending to be someone else then it is impossible to act naturally. This creates tension, hinders performance and gets in the way of good judgement. Good managers trust their instincts and act on their intuition. Work will always be stressful as long as your work persona is different from your natural self.

It is important to clarify the relationship between authenticity and modelling. Modelling excellence does not mean taking on all the characteristics of someone from whom you wish to learn. It is counter-productive to take on any characteristics that make you feel false. Use the modelling techniques to add to and enhance your own abilities rather than replace them with something completely alien.

Managing emotions

Our ability to manage pressure is a function of our emotional state. Emotions are the way we feel and, although commonly thought of as a 'mental subject', our emotional state is a physical state. We talk about feelings when we mean emotions. To help manage stress we need to remember that our brains govern how we think and our bodies govern how we feel. The way we stand, the way we breathe and the way we sit are all linked to our emotional state. Our physiology changes dramatically when our emotions change from being happy to being sad or vice versa.

At the beginning of this chapter we discussed how the body teaches the mind to feel. The reverse is also true, and our physiology changes in response to our thoughts. Take a moment to think about being sad and depressed or unhappy. Close your eyes and think about an unhappy event or experience. Now notice how you're sitting. If you're like most people, your shoulders will drop and your back will bend forward, your head will be down and, although your eyes are closed, they will be facing the floor. Your elbows and arms might have moved in towards your body, and your breathing will be slightly quicker than normal. Now change your mood and think about a really happy, joyous event. Try and get a clear picture of a time when you felt really on top of the world. Notice how your posture changes. Your shoulders will automatically be back, your head will be upright, your arms will have moved away from your body and you will be breathing more slowly: your whole posture will change.

If you have difficulty seeing the relationship between mood and physiology in adults, notice how mood affects children. Their bodies are a clear reflection of their mood. When a child is upset, it bends forward, puts its head down, shuffles forward. When children are happy, they stand up straight, smile and put their heads back. Younger children hop and skip, and radiate happiness. Perhaps the point when grown-ups stop skipping is when they start suffering from stress. The fact that our emotions are so closely linked to our physiology gives us a very powerful technique for helping to manage pressure. It's simply not possible to feel depressed, upset and unhappy when we stand upright, put our shoulders back, look up and smile. We may feel foolish doing it but it will help us feel better.

Figure 19: Managing Emotions*

Emotional Detachment

Emotions are hard to manage. Some people seem to keep their emotions under very tight rein. They appear to be cold, aloof and detached. Nothing seems to get them worked up and they go through life like robots. Other people are fiery, temperamental and excitable. The smallest incident sends them into extremes of anger or delight and we are never sure how they will react to a particular situation.

Everyone's emotional range is different. Some of us hover around a neutral point; others have wild mood swings. Some people tend to look on the black side and their emotional range seems to go from disappointment to depression. Other people have a much more positive approach to life and their positive, happy-go-lucky enthusiasms can sometimes seem overbearing.

Whatever our emotional range, we need to consider the extent to which we react emotionally to pressure and the impact this has on our stress levels.

Think about a situation where someone loses their temper with

---

* Peanuts cartoon ©1960 United Features Syndicate, Inc. Reproduced by permission.

you. It doesn't matter if their anger is justified or not. You are in a situation where somebody's getting angry and their anger is directed at you. How do you react? People tend to behave differently, depending on whether the incident was at work or outside of work. Outside of work you have fewer constraints and can react more naturally. At work the rules are different. You cannot shout back at customers or managers and you have to keep your feelings under control.

We need to learn to deal with these situations by being detached from what is happening and not letting it get to us. It's hard to avoid being hurt but it doesn't help to carry feelings of anger and being hurt around with us when the incident is over. One way of doing this is to picture ourselves stepping aside from our bodies while this is going on and think about what the exchange is saying about the people involved. If someone loses their temper with you and is abusive or aggressive then that is their problem, not yours. They might be equally unpleasant with anyone and the issue is about them, not about you. In this way you can see yourself as an objective, dispassionate bystander. You can keep calm, you can keep in control and you can avoid being hurt. The next time you're in this situation, just remember; it is not your problem.

Keep emotions current

The final point on managing emotions is to make sure you keep them up to date. Unless you're in a situation where you really cannot let yourself be yourself, you should always try to let your emotions be as natural as possible. Be yourself. You don't have to carry around an excess of emotional baggage from previous encounters. You can react to a situation in the most natural and appropriate way, and let yourself feel the appropriate emotion.

Many of us find it hard to keep in touch with our feelings. We may not be able to express them in a work or social context, but we shouldn't ignore the fact that they are there. Sometimes understanding that we are acting in a certain way because we are hurt by something makes it easier for us to come to terms with what we are doing.

8

Organisational Pressure

Tony is a business systems manager within the computing department of a large retail company. He has a first-class degree from Cambridge and at the age of 34 has been identified as someone who is going places. Up to now he's been mainly involved in technical roles and hasn't had much experience of 'people' management. He has run a few project teams but they've always disbanded when the project finished. Tony is bright, dynamic and aggressive. He's extremely ambitious and determined to get to the top. Tony firmly believes he's a first-rate manager. He thinks that his people like and respect him, and although he puts them under a lot of pressure, he thinks it's good for them and that they enjoy it.

His current project is hitting trouble at the moment. It's the biggest and longest project he's been responsible for and its on-time delivery is vital to the company's business needs. Unfortunately, the project is slipping. Tony's working longer and longer hours, and driving his people as hard as he can to get them to make up lost time. Some of the problems aren't his fault. Two of his team are off on long-term sick leave and Tony's written them off because he doesn't think they can stand the pressure. He's had two or three resignations over the last three months and a couple of other people have told him they want to transfer to other departments.

Tony thinks he could manage the labour turnover, but he can't get anyone to transfer into his project team. They all seem to have some excuse about being tied up with their current projects. Someone from personnel tried to talk to him about problems in his team, but Tony thinks she doesn't understand what it's like to work on an important, complex project.

Tony knows he sets very high standards for himself and other people, and it's not his fault that the stuff his team produces has to be done over and over again because it isn't good enough. He's starting to get a bit worried about the delays though. His boss has talked to him a few times recently about working his people too hard and the fact that the project keeps missing the delivery deadlines.

Tony's project is doomed to failure and his career is going to take a major knock. By loading pressure on his people and exposing them to the frustrations of the customers, he is making their lives impossible. Tony forgets that, like him, they want the project to succeed. They want to do their best for the customers but they need clear priorities, a good environment and a stationary target. The last thing they need when they're trying to do a difficult job is for their manager to come into the office and dump his stress all over them. They have enough of their own without Tony adding to the pile.

Tony may be good at the technical aspects of his job, but he isn't good at managing people. Tony has created many of his own problems by acting as a stress amplifier. He knows the project is important, and he's put under pressure by his bosses and the user departments to deliver good quality products on time. Unfortunately, Tony takes every bit of pressure, magnifies it and feeds it back to his staff. Small problems or trivial requests for changes become major issues. He is eager to please and desperately keen to succeed, but he's doing so at the expense of the people who work for him. They can only work so hard and take so much. Tony needs to learn how to absorb stress, and act as a buffer between his sources of pressure and his people.

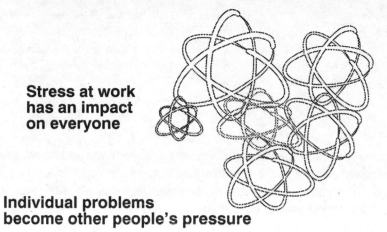

**Stress at work
has an impact
on everyone**

**Individual problems
become other people's pressure**

Figure 20: Stress Chain Reaction

We conducted a stress audit and identified a group of managers who were clearly better at managing stress than their colleagues. When we investigated further we found that one of the major reasons they felt they could manage stress was because they thought it was part of their job. It went with the territory. These managers instinctively knew that their role meant being a stress buffer, not a stress carrier.

MANAGING OTHER PEOPLE'S PRESSURE

Clear goals

All good performance starts with clear goals. We need to be aware of the assumptions we make about the level of understanding of the people who work for us, and we need to be conscious of how much we need to clarify and explain. Over and over again managers make the classic mistake of telling people what tasks to perform rather than what they want them to achieve. We may need to go into detail and explain, sometimes step by step, precisely what we require, but we should do this in the context of what we want.

A friend of mine, a management consultant, was talking about how pleased he was with the work the builders had done on his house. He hadn't had the usual problems with the work going over budget, not being done properly and all the other difficulties people get into when dealing with builders. The secret of his success was very simple. 'I specified the outputs, not the inputs.' In any job, whether it's something people are doing for us, things we are doing for ourselves or things we're doing for other people, it's what we achieve that matters, not the steps we took to achieve it. There is never just one way of doing something and concentrating on the inputs, the steps that we take to produce the desired result, misses the point. If I want someone to go out of the door on my right it's much easier to show them the door and let them make their own way out, than try and tell them the steps they have to take to get there. Anyone who has tried to write even the simplest computer programme knows this problem. If you insist on specifying the inputs you have to be very, very good to get the output you desire. It's so much easier to tell people what you want them to achieve and let them get on with it.

Other people's pressure

Problems cause pressure. Our natural reaction, when faced with a problem, is to perceive it as a threat. In many situations what has happened isn't our problem at all. You may, for example, feel let down because someone didn't do something as expected. If you see that as your problem, you'll put yourself under pressure trying to deal with it. It's far easier and far more effective to pass the problem back to the person who has let you down. Simply saying 'It's not my problem, it's yours, what are you going to do about it'? achieves two benefits. First, it stops you worrying about the issue and, secondly, by bouncing the problem firmly back to the person who was trying to make it yours, they are more likely to do something to put matters right. We do not have to take on other people's problems unless we want to. Learn to reflect or deflect other people's pressure.

Managing the monkey

The benefits of not taking other people's problems on board have been described in the book, *The One Minute Manager Meets the Monkey*, by Dr Ken Blanchard, William Oncken and Hal Burrows.[1] In this book, part of his excellent One Minute Manager series, Blanchard describes someone with a problem as someone with a monkey on their back. What they are trying to do is to get rid of their problem by getting you to take the monkey. As soon as they can do that, the monkey (that is to say, the problem) is off their back and they're free to carry on doing their job without having to worry about this particular problem. Blanchard advises his readers to make sure that when the person who came with the problem leaves, the monkey is still on their back. If you're a manager, you coach and advise your staff on how to deal with the monkey but, and this is the key point, you don't solve the problem for them. You make absolutely sure that they understand that it's their monkey and they have to deal with it.

Like many of these techniques for managing pressure, the principle is just as important at home as it is at work. Children expect their parents to take the monkey off them. Sometimes you may need to; other times they may learn a lot by solving their own problems. Don't take the monkey unless you want it.

MANAGING INDIVIDUALS

Traditional management training emphasises the logical, rational, analytical process. The subject of management studies is frequently called management sciences and many university departments are proud of their management science schools. Unfortunately, people do not lend themselves easily to being the subjects of scientific analysis or scientific management.

Managers should also look out for the signs of stress, described in Chapter 2, to make sure they are not overloading their staff. Different people have widely differing tolerances of uncertainty. Some people need guidance, while others need independence. Managers should recognise that one person's job autonomy is another's role ambiguity.

As managers, we ought to know how our employees will respond to pressure. We need to make sure that we recognise and appreciate the individual differences in our staff, our colleagues and even our superiors. Most of the time we're too busy and too preoccupied with our own stress, and our own lives, that we fail to appreciate other people's perceptions. If we thought about it, we probably already have the information and know how people are likely to respond to a given situation, but we simply don't think about it.

People are individuals. They are inconsistent, idiosyncratic, emotional, wilful and unpredictable. The argument that, although you may not be able to predict the behaviour of one person, you can predict the behaviour of groups, is completely irrelevant in the management of people. Managing people is about managing individuals, not about managing groups, and the person at the receiving end of your management style is an individual, not a member of a group. Trying to apply 'scientific management' to individuals will create pressure for you and your employees.

We need to take the management principles we learn through training programmes or university courses and test them in the real world on real people. If they don't work, it's not the person that's wrong, it's the principle. Unfortunately, in many organisations, if people don't respond to being managed in a certain way they leave. They find themselves on the redundancy list, they're transferred to other jobs or they simply get so fed up that they resign. We need to be much more flexible and more free-thinking in our approach to managing people.

Chapter 1 showed the pressure – performance curve. Managers should think of the optimum range of pressure for each of their employees and try to make sure that they stay at an optimal level. Some of the behavioural clues of optimum performance are:

- energy and enthusiasm;

- alertness;

- high morale;

- good humour;

- cheerfulness;

- positive, can do approach;

- calmness;

- quick decision making.

A manager with five people working for her will probably need at least five different management styles, each of which is tailored to the needs of the particular employee. In practice, the manager may need more than five styles because people change and are inconsistent. The soft, sympathetic approach may work with one person on one day, but a completely different approach may be required the next day. We must get away from the feeling that there is a 'right way to manage'. Think carefully about the people who work for you, and identify their particular needs and motivation.

Traditional management thinking tries to get people to conform to a pattern or a 'type'. Think about this in terms of the way that you are managed. Would you rather be managed as a type or as a person? We need structure to make sense of the world but over-reliance on structure is damaging and stressful. People don't fit into neat boxes with simple labels and we should not try to make them.

We have already seen that two of the major causes of stress in organisations are bad bosses and poor communications. It is possible that one of the reasons for this is the inappropriateness of management training that teaches managers to manage 'categories' of people rather than individuals. The worst examples of bad management are found in those managers and supervisors who treat people as objects. They manage people in the same way that a process worker manages filling a box of chocolates. They move people around without explanation, give them jobs to do without explaining why they're doing them and ignore any signs of humanity. Clear communication is only possible when you deal with people as individuals.

> Vera worked as a packer in a cheese factory. She and 100 other people would arrive at the early shift at 6.00 am and be allocated jobs by the supervisor. There was no greeting and no warmth. Vera would just be told to 'Get over there' or 'Work on that machine'. There was no element of choice, no regard for social groups, variety, job rotation or anything. John, the supervisor, treated the people like units of production. He assigned people to machines in exactly the same way as he allocated materials. Vera and the other production workers hated their jobs, and hated the supervisor. They didn't particularly mind that their jobs were cold, greasy, dirty and unpleasant, what they minded was being treated without respect.

The interesting feature about this story is that John, the supervisor, isn't a cruel person, nor is he unfeeling. He loves his wife and family, is the leading light in the local amateur dramatics society, and is always willing to turn out and help in the aid of a good cause. John doesn't treat the workers badly because he wants to, but because he's being 'efficient'. He joined the dairy company straight from school as a packer, and worked with Vera and the others on the production lines. His only model for how to manage was his supervisor. So, when John was promoted to assistant charge-hand and then supervisor, he simply copied the model that he knew. He was proud of improving productivity and accepted that being disliked went with the job. John had been on a couple of training courses but found 'they were interesting but not really relevant to my situation here at the dairy.'

There are probably tens of thousands of Johns working in supervisory or management roles in organisations throughout the country. They do their jobs and, for the most part they do them quite well, but they're not happy in what they do and feel under pressure as a result of their managerial role and their relationships with other people. They don't all behave as coldly or as unfeelingly towards their staff as John but the gap is still there They are not communicating with their people and they never will, until they learn to treat people as individuals and give them the respect that they deserve.

Alienation and lack of control

Lack of control is a major problem for many people in organisations. Many people feel that they have no control over their organisation or their work environment and very little opportunity for individual influence. This problem is most acute lower down the organisation where shop floor workers, administrative staff and others really have no control at all.

The problem is particularly bad in production line work where people are controlled by the machine. They work at the rate of the production process and do specific tasks under the control of a supervisor. There is little control in the job and no real sense of value. This lack of control is one of the reasons why stress is worse for blue-collar workers than white-collar workers.

We need to find ways to maximise the level of control and influence we have in our jobs. It may only happen in small ways, but there should be things that people can do which allow them to use a little more judgement or take a bit more responsibility. Organisations that fail to encourage their employees to take control are seriously under-utilising their most valuable resource. In the worst case, lack of control doesn't simply waste talent, it can create an environment in which employees' creative energies have no legitimate means of expression and are used to disrupt and damage the business instead.

Charles Denby writes about his experiences on the production line in Detroit, in *Indignant Heart, Testimony of a Black American Worker*.[2] Denby gives a graphic description of the things people did to stop the production line.

> As long as we are mad at the set-up one of us can keep one (welding) gun out of action all the time ... if they make us work without any time off then we wreck a gun and take a few minutes while it is being repaired. This happens all through the shop. Many times the guns could be easily repaired. A worker sees his gun going bad. He has no interest in saving it so he'll let it go completely wrong and burn clear up before calling the repairman. Many times we know what is wrong and if we feel really good we repair it ourselves. The workers put things in their guns or break them on purpose. (p 140)

Sabotaging production was the only way in which these workers could exercise any degree of influence or control in their jobs. The American car makers might have avoided some of their labour disputes if they had used the energies and talents of their employees creatively, instead of making them work in situations where they have no control and the only outlet for their talents is destructive.

> If the workers are real mad they will jam up the line by putting something in it or jimmying some part. The repairman won't be able to find out what is wrong. After a rest one of us will fix it and the line rolls again.[3]

Think of how many millions of dollars must have been lost through this sort of behaviour. Workers being so angry at the way they are treated they have to find ways of stopping production. As Denby says: 'The company never gets full production.' The workers have managed, despite a strict autocratic management, to gain control. They decide when and how fast the line will run. Everyone needs to feel in control, if the company takes it away they will find a way of getting it back. Denby is writing about extreme behaviour, but we see subtle examples of the need for control in almost every organisation. It might be adding a few more minutes to the lunch break, not wearing hearing protection or insisting on doing a job their way despite being told the 'right' way. Fortunately, there are signs that industry is changing and managers have finally woken up to the fact that people cannot be treated like machines.

Job insecurity

The recession of the 1980s has made the notion of secure employment a nonsense. No one is safe when the world's largest and most successful organisations start making people redundant, downsizing and delayering. Not that many years ago, people would join organisations like the Civil Service expecting to have a job for life. They could be assured of a steady, secure, stable and even predictable career. Providing they did reasonably well they could expect a number of promotions, a reasonable rate of pay and an excellent pension. With the arrival of contracting out of services, privatisation of public sector organisations and 'market testing', the world of the civil servant has changed dramatically in a few short years. Organisations can no longer guarantee a job for life and the lack of job security can be a major, ongoing source of pressure for many people.

Lack of security is particularly acute for people in their mid-twenties to late thirties. With the decline in the housing market, many of them have 'negative equity'. They have borrowed more on the mortgage than the house is worth. Even if they could sell the house, they would not have enough to pay back the money they borrowed to buy it. They have growing families and need to maintain a certain level of income. They all know at least one person who has been made redundant and the threat of losing their job through no fault of their own can provide a constant, unsettling background to their working week. There are no safe havens and there is no job security. Loyalty to an employer has to be replaced by mutual respect and people need to plan their lives on the basis of probable risks rather than preserving the status quo.

Constant organisational change and restructuring means that even if a company or department is doing well it is always possible that a reorganisation may result in the removal of a layer of management or a complete function. The middle manager in the 1990s is an endangered species. The gurus of organisational change keep telling employers that they don't need middle managers any more and that they should get rid of every part of the business that isn't critical to its survival. Administration, personnel, financial, legal and other departments are all under threat. Organisations can get sub-contractors to provide all of these services. Even skilled and semi-skilled manual work can be sub-contracted.

The recession has forced many organisations to re-evaluate their employment practices, and they have become leaner and fitter. They have learnt new ways of working and found more efficient ways of getting people to do the work. One example of changing work practices is the reliance on 'temporary workers'. People are recruited for specific projects on either rolling or fixed length contracts. They have no continuity of employment and, over the past few years, have replaced a large number of permanent staff. After an organisation has discovered that it can get rid of 50 per cent of its managers and continue to function, there is no way it will replace the lost jobs when the recession ends. On the shop floor level, when a company finds it can reduce its labour force by 30 per cent and, at the same time, increase output per person by 10 per cent it will continue to look for ways of improving productivity rather than, as in the past, throwing people at the problem.

PRESSURE AND PERFORMANCE AT WORK

We are capable of producing extraordinary performance under pressure. Tom Peters, the management guru and co-author of *In Search of Excellence*, frequently talks about people producing out-standing performance as a result of impossible demands placed upon them by their managers. His studies of excellence show that quite often, when people ask for the impossible, they get it. Peters cites many examples of people inspiring themselves and others to achieve incredible goals, by setting challenging targets and creating pressure.[4]

We need to manage the pressure process for ourselves and, if we have any staff responsibility, we need to help manage it for the people who work for us. Managing pressure doesn't get mentioned very often in books on management techniques, but in many ways it is the essence of good management. It is also very difficult to do. Each of us has a pressure band that produces optimum perfor-mance. Some people may be able to tolerate a wide range of pressure. Others are more vulnerable. The individual differences in the way we respond to and manage pressure are discussed in more detail in Chapter 3.

Reward and recognition

We change people's behaviours by positive reinforcement. The carrot is more powerful than the stick in achieving the extra push that makes the difference between the adequate and the excellent.

One of the most rewarding ways of managing pressure is through the use of praise and recognition. All of us, no matter how cynical, need positive feedback. We need to know how we are doing and we need people to emphasise the positive, not the negative. Knowing other people care about us and value us gives us strength, and helps us to deal with pressure. If we know that we are OK then we can deal with our problems; if we doubt our self-worth we start to believe that we are the problem and fail to manage pressure effectively.

One way of understanding more about our need for affection is to think about stroking (see the section on Transactional Analysis in Chapter 6, where the need for stroking is discussed). We show affection for and reward our dog or our cat by giving it pats or stroking it. Our pet knows that it is loved and cared for, and responds by letting us know how much it enjoys our demonstration of affection. Unfortunately we are not very good at doing the same thing with people. We tend to be quite reserved and stroking people on the shop floor, and giving them pats and hugs, is not normally regarded as acceptable behaviour!

However, the need to let people know we care about them is very important and, if we cannot stroke them physically, we should do it verbally. We need to make sure that we thank them and praise people for what they have done, and show them that we recognise their efforts and achievements.

We should not do this in a false or artificial way because doing that makes the stroking meaningless. The ubiquitous 'Have a nice day' that we hear in American shops when said without feeling becomes an annoyance and an irritation. Empty stroking, doing it for the sake of doing it without really meaning it, can be patronising and insulting, and should be avoided. There is always something positive to say about someone and we should try to make more of an effort to let them know we value them.

Praising doesn't need to be elaborate or over the top. It can, at its easiest level, be simple recognition: 'Thank you for getting that job in to me on time, I really appreciate your efforts. Well done'. Those few brief words, sincerely meant, can make all the hard work and effort that went into a particular task seem worth while. Many people find that the job isn't properly finished until it has been recognised and acknowledged.

People need recognition. We cannot run businesses by treating people as units of production. We have to treat them as individuals, and be aware of their needs and desires, moods and motivations, and so on. The absentee manager who sits in his ivory tower surrounded by papers, computer printouts and telephones, and never deals with his people as people is, quite rightly, a doomed species. Managers have to know their people and be known by them. They should be approachable, accessible and available.

The majority of managers are poor at praising their staff and giving them the appropriate recognition for good performance. However, when we asked managers in an organisation to tell us how often they praise people, most replied that they recognise good performance on a weekly, if not daily, basis. For some reason, the people who work for them don't seem to be getting the message. Very few of the subordinates of these managers said they had been praised.

We know that people respond well to positive reinforcement. The well known Hawthorne Experiment conducted by Elton Mayo showed that productivity is more affected by attitude and feelings than the working environment. Mayo monitored a group of workers at the Hawthorne plant of the Western Electricity Company to see if changing the lighting levels increased their productivity. The experiment showed that when lighting levels were increased, productivity went up, and the researchers thought that they had established a simple way to increase output and sell more electricity. They were somewhat surprised when they reduced the lighting level again to discover that productivity continued to go up.

The researchers realised that what was making the difference to the group was not the change in the lighting, but the fact that people were showing an interest in the workers. In effect, the workers were being stimulated, being shown that somebody actually cared about them and they responded positively. Mayo's experiment demonstrated that taking an interest in people is an extremely effective morale booster. It also prompted Tom Peters to declare that managers needed to create more Hawthorne effects.

Creating Hawthorne Effects

As an example of what can be done to manage organisational pressure, BNL Ltd, a small plastic bearings manufacturer based in North Yorkshire, has put an enormous amount of effort into improving communications since the business was bought out from an industrial group. Before the buyout BNL epitomised poor organisational communication. Although only employing 110 people, the business was highly fragmented, production didn't talk to sales, finance was ignored and everything was always a crisis or a problem. The business had suffered very badly from a lack of direction and a divided management team. People were under pressure and stress levels were high. BNL recognised the problem and the damage it was doing to their workforce, and their ability to survive and prosper in an extremely competitive market place. The company decided to act and introduced a series of simple measures designed to involve people at all levels of the business.

None of the things they have done are particularly revolutionary and none of them have involved any major expenditure. Some of the actions they have taken are as follows.

- *Introduction of coffee mornings*   Three times a week, from 9.30 to 10.00 am the managers, directors and some specialist technical staff come together in the MD's office for coffee. These sessions are completely informal and are designed simply to let people find out what's going on throughout the rest of the business. The coffee mornings take place irrespective of the MD being there and, after some initial scepticism and being seen as a waste of time, they are now regarded as an essential part of running the business. People stand during the coffee morning, so conversations tend to be brief and to the point.   As a consequence, the number of formal meetings has been reduced, leaving more time for people to do their jobs rather than attend meetings and the increased level of understanding and co-operation between the different departments has prevented many potential problems from occurring.

- *Team briefings*   Briefing meetings have been around for a long time and organisations such as the Industrial Society have successfully introduced them into many organisations. At BNL, the briefing meetings are managed by the quality manager and the marketing manager. They combine their skills to produce punchy, effective briefings. They recognise that most briefing groups fail because they get stale and boring. At BNL, they keep changing the briefer, rotate the groups, let different people deliver different parts of the brief and so on. Not all of their ideas work as well as others, but the message gets across and the staff benefit from the experience. The quality of the briefings has improved steadily over the year and, having started with questions about matters such as the colour of the toilet wall or the state of the car park, they are now receiving high quality suggestions for improvements, and interesting and informed questions about future policies of the business.

- *Work experience*   To help people understand more about the work in other departments, the company has introduced a 'How BNL Works' scheme. This allows people to spend a week gaining experience in other departments. The programme is entirely voluntary and within a few weeks of being launched they have already had requests from over half the employees to go on the programme.

Pressure in the organisation has reduced because people know what's going on and do not feel threatened by fear of the unknown or the unexpected. The business responds rapidly to the needs of its customers and, instead of lurching from crisis to crisis, they are now much better able to anticipate problems and prevent them occurring

BNL's hard work in involving their employees has been done, wherever possible, in a light-hearted and humorous way. In the face of severe recession in all of its markets, BNL has succeeded in beating its budget targets and has continued to grow.

Many organisations are taking similar steps to improve the fundamental nature of communication between themselves and their employees. They are no longer taking people for granted and recognise that they need to continue being innovative in their approach to improvement. Companies don't need to spend a fortune on improving their communication processes. They simply need to think about the way they treat their people, decide to do it better and work very hard to make sure that it doesn't become stale.

Managing by respect

There are thousands of management books describing a wide range of management processes. They cover management by results, management by objectives, management by design and so on. Unfortunately, very little is said about management by respect. Management by respect starts with the premise that everyone, whatever their role in the organisation, from the most humble to the most exalted, is worthy of respect. Everyone has a contribution to make, and people will be most effective if their specific abilities and skills are recognised and acknowledged. Management by respect treats people positively. It assumes that people are capable and conscientious, and will give their best if they are treated as responsible and interested human beings.

Management by respect is the basis for empowerment and empowerment programmes are doomed to failure unless the attitude of management towards their staff and staff towards management is built on a foundation of mutual respect. The difficulty of managing by respect is that respect cannot be bought; it has to be earned. We have already seen that there is no one way of managing people and that people have to be treated as individuals. Managing by respect recognises this and accepts a wide range of management styles. It doesn't necessarily mean that an employer has to be open, sharing and communicative. Employees can have respect for managers who may be hard, tough minded and perhaps even unfair. What they can respect about these managers may be the amount of effort they put into projects, their leadership qualities, their marketing flair or whatever. What hard-nosed, hard-edged managers, who would be deeply offended if anyone thought them 'people people' have is respect for their staff. Their respect, their commitment, their productivity, their interest in quality and so on. Anyone can manage by respect. It doesn't need an MBA or extensive training. It simply requires that we look for the good in people and treat them as human beings.

The principles of managing by respect can be applied to every aspect of life. At work, you can respect your colleagues, your customers and even your suppliers. You should think about people as people, not as a means to achieving an end. The curious thing about respecting people and being conscious of doing so is that it will make it easier for other people to respect you. If you treat people as you would like to be treated, then you will be.

Participation

We have suggested that employees will be able to manage pressure more effectively if they are given more control over their working environment. However, we should be careful that we don't simply play at participation and tell the staff that they are 'empowered' without actually changing their ability to get things done. In our consultancy work, we see many examples of organisations who claim that they have introduced employee involvement, continuous improvement or other participative programmes. In practice, they have spent their time and money on a PR exercise which allows groups of workers to meet together outside the normal management structures and perhaps suggest some ideas. All that happens in these situations is that the employees quickly discover that they have no real power and, ultimately, all the important decisions affecting their work and working environment are still made through the same managerial hierarchies. Participation needs to be practised, not preached.

These are the people who came to work to earn their money, spend some time with their mates and want the minimum involvement for the maximum pay. They don't want to think; they simply want to be told what to do. These views can be very strongly held and, if someone chooses not to become involved in a participation programme, then their choice must be respected. Our experience suggests that, given time, a number of these people start to see the benefits of the programme, and change their attitude but, as one of the supervisors in a steel buildings factory said at the time an improvement programme was introduced, 'I'm not interested in worrying about the company's problems, I've got enough problems of my own. All I want is to come to work, do my job then go home. The last thing I want to do is think about how I can help the company to improve.' There will always be a group of employees who simply don't want to get involved. These people are often employees who work on repetitive tasks with little opportunity to exercise flexibility. For these employees, an involvement programme may simply add to the levels of frustration they already feel.

Although it is possible to impose an empowerment programme on the workforce it makes a nonsense of the principles of involvement if employees have to be forced to take part. Organisations need to create a climate where employees understand the benefits to them and the organisation of greater involvement, and want to become actively involved in the programme. Often, a quiet, low key approach, implemented on a departmental basis, can achieve far better and longer lasting results than a major employee involvement programme that fails to address the real issues.

Involvement programmes can also threaten managers. The steel buildings supervisor commented 'I've worked bloody hard to get where I am, I enjoy telling people what to do and I'm not going to start asking them for their ideas.' Fortunately, this level of resistance is rare, but its existence needs to be recognised. Interestingly, the supervisor who was so opposed to the scheme in the first place became one of the programme's strongest champions when he realised how useful the programme was in improving productivity.

Involvement and participation programmes work because they increase the employee's sense of control. The employee is no longer helpless in the face of rapid changes in the workplace but can directly or indirectly influence them. The involvement programmes can also reduce role conflict and ambiguity. The more time and trouble organisations take to help their employees understand the contributions they can make to the success of the organisation, the more opportunity there is for employees to clarify their roles. They also have less difficulty with conflicting priorities. If you understand the key success factors for an organisation then the decision whether to do job X or job Y is easier to make. For many people, role conflict and task conflict is caused by a failure to understand the organisation's objectives and the part they can play in achieving them.

Flexible working

One of the easiest ways of improving an employee's ability to influence and control their working environment is to introduce flexible working schemes. These include programmes such as flexitime or variable work patterns, job sharing, career breaks, and teleworking. Simple flexitime programmes allow employees to choose their start and finish times within certain pre-determined limits. Starting at 7.00 a.m. and finishing at 4.00 p.m. may help someone to avoid the traffic and spend a bit more time with their family. More sophisticated flexible working schemes enable employees to choose where and when to work. This form of flexible working is sometimes known as teleworking or location independent working. The number of people on flexible working schemes is growing rapidly and, as of 1993, almost 5 per cent of the UK workforce was involved in remote working. A large number of organisations are actively promoting flexible working schemes in an attempt to reduce office costs whilst improving productivity and efficiency. One of the leading companies in this field is Mercury Communications Ltd which, as a telecoms company, is keen to use the technology to enable people to choose their place of work. Mercury has established a flexible working group to help their own staff to make the transition to flexible or location independent working. This group also provides a range of services to assist other organisations, in the public and private sector, to set up flexible working schemes.

The move towards flexible working can be traumatic both for the individual and the organisation. Like all organisational change, flexible working needs to be managed effectively if it is to produce the desired benefits. As the technology required to enable people to work remotely becomes cheaper and easier to use, the number of people making the transition to location independent working will increase dramatically. This change in working practices will have profound implications for the individual, the family and society as a whole, as well as for the world of work. Flexible working has encouraged the development of a new breed of 'open collar' workers. These people may have the ultimate control over their organisation. Recent years have seen the development of 'virtual corporations', and the growth of informal networks. Loose coalitions of freelances working as associates on specific projects will be one of the major features of employment as we move towards the end of the century.

References

1   Blanchard, K, Oncken, W and Burrows, H (1983) *The One Minute Manager Meets the Monkey:* Fontana, London.

2   Denby, C (1978) *Indignant Heart, Testimony of a Black American Worker:* South End Press, Boston, Mass.

3   Denby, C, op cit.

4   Peters, T, Waterman, R (1983) *In Search of Excellence:* Harper and Row, New York.

9

Making a Difference

James is a senior manager in the marketing department of a large leisure company. He was recruited with the objective of transforming a moribund and inefficient department that had been ticking over for years. James rose to the challenge and tackled his job with vigour. He got involved in the details of the projects, recruited some new people, built better links to the rest of the company, brought in a new advertising agency and, in 18 months, completely transformed the marketing function. James was tired but exhilarated. He had the satisfaction of knowing he had done a good job and, although he hadn't seen much of his wife and kids for the last 18 months, he thought it had been worth it.

About six months ago, James came to a managing pressure programme I was running for his company. During the session James completed an Occupational Stress Indicator questionnaire (OSI) and we spent half an hour talking about his stress profile. The next time I met James was about four months later when he told me I had changed his life. I hadn't done anything of the kind, but James had. He had looked carefully at his OSI results and thought about some of the issues. The OSI showed that he had a problem with the interface between home and work and, although he was highly satisfied with his job, he was under some pressure from his managerial role and didn't really feel he had as much control as he would like. James was using a reasonably good range of coping mechanisms but his time management and social support skills were definitely under-utilised.

James had taken all this on board, and applied the same determination, decisiveness and energy to sorting out his life that he applied to sorting out the department. He went home early on the night of the seminar and had a long talk to his wife about the hours he had been working and his desire to spend more time at home. The next day he booked a holiday. He hadn't really had time for more than a few days' holiday during the previous 18 months so he took 2 weeks to get away with his wife and kids. When he came back, he booked himself on a time management and a delegation skills course, and went on both of those within three weeks of his return from holiday.

Since that time, James has been going home at a reasonable hour every night. He still has to travel a lot and there are occasions when he needs to work late but, on average, he's been spending more time with his family than he has done for years. He's also improved his management skills and has started to delegate effectively. His staff already thought he was a good manager and now they like him even more. The 'new' James gives them more responsibility and they get more satisfaction out of their jobs.

I asked James to complete another OSI to see if I could see any changes in his stress profile. The second profile accurately reflected the improvements that James had made in managing pressure. The home/work interface was better. He was making more use of time management and social support skills. His mental and physical health had improved, and his job satisfaction levels had increased even further. The last time I saw him, James had just been promoted to marketing director. He would have got there anyway but now, with his improved ability to manage pressure, he has the spare capacity he needs to make another success of a bigger job.

James's story isn't a fairy tale. It is a true story of someone who recognised the need for change, accepted the responsibility for change and took the appropriate action. James is fortunate. As a senior manager he was able to organise a holiday and training courses when he wanted them. He had more freedom to change his life than many other people, but what James did can be done by anyone. The improvement may not be quite so dramatic or as quick, but it can be done. All it takes is an awareness of the need for change, the motivation to change, the acceptance of responsibility and action.

A sales assistant working on a checkout in a supermarket achieved a similar fundamental change in her life by thinking about what she wanted, understanding what she needed to do and doing something about it. She didn't book a holiday or a training course, but she changed her approach to work and her relationship with her boyfriend. There are no barriers to change if you want to do it. In the words of the old proverb, 'Where there's a will, there's a way'.

INTERVENTIONS

We can improve our ability to manage pressure in a wide variety of ways. There are no single solutions to managing pressure, and we need to use an ever changing and broad based range of techniques to continue to improve.

> The wheel is turning and you can't slow down
> You can't let go and you can't hold on
> You can't go back and you can't stand still,
> If the thunder don't get you, then the lightning will.
>
> Won't you try just a little bit harder
> Couldn't you try just a little bit more*.

In this book we've looked at many techniques for managing pressure at an individual level. We can improve our personal ability to manage pressure, but we get the maximum benefit from an

---

* Words and Music by Garcia, Hunter and Kreutzman ©1972 Ice Nine Pub, USA
  Warner Chappell Music Ltd, London W1Y 3FA
  Reproduced by permission of International Music Publications Ltd.

integrated approach that includes organisational and managerial, as well as individual, initiatives.

Organisational interventions

Improve communications

Clear and effective communications are the key to removing pressure and improving effectiveness. Think of how productive your organisation would be if all communications between your managers and employees, and customers and suppliers, were clear and precise. There would be no false assumptions, no wasted work, and everyone understanding and working in harmony with each other to a common purpose. It may be an idealistic dream but even a small improvement in the clarity of communication will produce massive benefits for everyone.

Develop or demote bad bosses

Bad managers do untold damage to organisations. They damage people, productivity and profitability. No organisation in its right mind would continue to run a machine that kept breaking or rejecting components, but organisations continue to employ, and even promote, managers who harm the lives of the people who work for them. Good managers do not have to be soft, inefficient or even particularly people oriented. They do need to understand their staff, be sensitive to their needs and give them the opportunity to grow. If they can't do that on their own, they should be trained and encouraged. If training fails they should do something else.

Review the organisation's structure

In a discontinuous world the organisational structure that worked in the 1960s and 1970s is probably inappropriate for the 1990s. It's worth making sure that your organisational structure is designed to meet the needs of the business both now and in the future. It should encourage freedom, flexibility and innovation, and ensure that it meets the needs of your customers. Organisational change is traumatic and often expensive. However, working in a dysfunctional organisation is even more frustrating and, in the long run, the price of failing is receivership.

Review working practices

One aspect of the way the world is changing is that full-time employees will soon be a minority. To what extent does your organisation recognise the structural changes in our society? What steps have you taken to make it easier for people to adopt flexible working practices, to encourage people returning to work, and recruit and train the older workers? Working practices, employment contracts and the whole relationship between employer and employee need to be reviewed to ensure that they continue to be appropriate.

Develop a participative culture

Rosabeth Moss Kanter believes that:

> The corporations that will succeed and flourish in the times ahead will be those that have mastered the art of change; creating a climate encouraging the introduction of new procedures and new possibilities, encouraging anticipation of and response to external pressures, encouraging and listening to new ideas from inside the organisation. (p 65)[1]

The need for control is central to managing pressure. Participation, devolved responsibility and guided self-help are all tools for helping individuals gain control and make an effective contribution to the organisation, while enhancing their own working lives.

Improve working conditions

People have enough to put up with at work without working in dirty, noisy, unpleasant or hazardous environments. Although this is the last on our list of organisational interventions, it's probably one of the most important. There's no point in having the world's best participative management system if people run the risk of being injured by the machines or poisoned by their environment. Your employees should be proud of their place of work, and want to bring their families and friends in to look around. Pride in the place of work encourages pride in the work itself and that encourages quality. The higher the quality, the lower the pressure.

Managerial interventions

Share the vision

As a manager, it is your responsibility to make sure that your staff understand the contributions they can make to the business. Like the stone-mason building the cathedral they should understand what they are really involved in; not the little bit of the business into which they have been compartmentalised or pigeon-holed.

They should know their role and the value it adds to the business, and not be exposed to the pressure of uncertainty.

Define objectives

People need clear goals and employees should understand the criteria against which their performance is being measured. Remember to specify objectives in terms of outputs, not inputs, and ensure that employees can monitor their own performance against their objectives.

Clarify roles

Ambiguity and uncertainty create an enormous amount of pressure. It's a fine line between job autonomy and role ambiguity. Managers need to help their staff to understand their role. Sharing the vision and defining the objectives will make a significant contribution towards clarification of roles, but managers need to go further than this, and make the link between an individual's job and the organisational goals explicit.

Delegate effectively

Bad delegation is bad for everyone. It's bad for the manager, bad for their staff and bad for the organisation. Managers should make sure that every job is done by the most junior person capable of doing that job successfully. This provides challenge and opportunities for growth for people lower down the organisation, and creates freedom and responsibility for people higher up. This objective may be difficult to achieve in rigid, bureaucratic organisations or organisations where risk and innovation are discouraged. As organisations become flatter and evolve into new, flexible structures, delegation skills will become even more important. Train all your managers to delegate now.

Recognise achievement

People thrive on praise. Recognising and acknowledging achievement is a wonderful motivator and helps the person being praised to feel a sense of completion. Be careful not to praise for the sake of praising, and try to keep the interval between someone doing a job well and having their achievement recognised as short as possible. Recognition doesn't need to take the form of monetary reward. A letter will be remembered long after the bonus has been spent.

Genuine recognition of achievement provides a positive reinforcement of successful behaviour. It helps develop winners. The other good thing about recognising achievement is that you will feel better for doing it. 'It's better to give than to receive', and it's very satisfying to know that you have genuinely recognised and acknowledged someone else's achievement.

Consider others

Managers work under pressure, and life can be difficult when we are struggling to meet budgets, achieve targets and make a contribution in a tough business climate. It's very easy under those circumstances to become preoccupied with ourselves. We need to take time to consider other people and be sensitive to their needs. This isn't just the people that work for us, though they are obviously important. It's the people that work around us, and our family and friends. Do you know the effect you have on the people around you? Do you know how the people who work for you feel about their jobs and about the way that they are managed? Do you recognise the problems that they may have as working mothers, people with major financial problems or elderly relatives? Thinking of other people and being sensitive to their needs shows that you respect and care for the people around you.

Make work fun

We spend a third of our waking lives at work – we ought to enjoy it. As managers we should create an atmosphere in which people can enjoy their work and have fun doing it. It's good for morale, it's good for growth and good for productivity. Look for the humour in situations, think about actions you can take to make work more enjoyable for your people and you'll find it more enjoyable for yourself.

Individual actions

Part 2 of this book has gone into some detail on the actions that you can take to help manage your pressure more effectively. The following checklist takes us back to the awareness, responsibility, action model we outlined at the beginning of the book and summarises the key steps in managing pressure.

Raise your awareness

Think about what's happening to you when you feel under stress, and get to know the feelings and the early warning signs that indicate when pressure is producing stress not growth. Over time, you will be able to pick up the signs and symptoms more easily, and be able to take appropriate action before the problems become too acute. The more you understand and the more sensitive you become to the ways in which you manage pressure, the more you will be aware of a need to take action and the more automatic the appropriate response.

Take responsibility

You are the only person who can manage your stress. Other people may be able to help but nobody can do it for you. Recognise that it's your responsibility and take control of managing your pressure. Managing pressure starts within you and is done by you. You are responsible for your own success.

Decide what you want

Think carefully and deeply about what you really want out of life. Remember, if in doubt ask yourself the key question, 'What do I value most in my life?' You need motivation to manage change actively and you have to find your motivation from a clear understanding of what you want.

Set realistic goals

We need to work towards goals that are achievable but represent a challenge. There is no point in fooling ourselves about our abilities but, at the same time, there's nothing worse than letting our self-limiting beliefs hold us back. We are all worth more than we think we are and we should recognise the danger of settling for too little in every aspect of our lives. It's better to try and fail, than never have tried at all, but we shouldn't set ourselves up for failure by ignoring the need for realistic goals.

Take action

When we know what we want and have set our targets, we need to take firm, decisive action to achieve our goals. We could spend the rest of our lives dreaming about a glorious future and still end up disappointed because we failed to translate thought into action. Nothing happens unless we act.

Make changes

'If you always do what you've always done, you'll always get what you've always got.' If we don't do anything different then nothing will change. The whole process of improving any aspect of our lives is to act differently. Improvement can only happen when things change.

Monitor progress

Throughout all the interventions we have described in this book, we need to maintain our awareness and our sensitivity to change. Are things getting better or worse? You have to find out what works for you and maximise your strengths. By monitoring progress you can keep checking to make sure that you are going in the right direction.

Managing pressure is achieved by doing things that feel right. Trust your judgement and, if it feels good and makes things better, then do more of it. If a particular programme or set of responses doesn't feel right to you then do something else. Suffering isn't good for you and it isn't necessary. Some of the activities and the changes you make to your life may initially be difficult, and any change is likely to create uncertainty and a temporary increase in pressure. If you're in control and you're doing things you believe to be right, then any negative effects should be brief and temporary. Managing pressure should be fun and should make you feel good. Focus on the positive, stay on track, keep improving and channel your energy into peak performance.

CONTINUOUS IMPROVEMENT

There are no right answers. You need to continue to learn and continue to improve. There is always a better way.

Changing direction and doing something different is, in itself, very positive. Every time you decide to do something differently, you take control. You make a decision and act upon it. It's a good habit to get into. Don't expect instant solutions. Our consumer society is built around the 'see it, want it, buy it' philosophy. 'We want the world and we want it now!' We expect goods to be available when we want to buy them, and fruits and vegetables to be in the supermarket all year round, regardless of the season. We apply this principle of instant gratification to changes in our lives. If we want to lose weight, we expect to go on an instant diet, or if we want to get fit we want it to happen straight away and without effort. Improving your ability to manage pressure takes time. There are no panaceas. It takes practice and perseverance to do it successfully. In improving your ability to manage pressure, do the easy things first and build on the positive feedback of success. Continue to improve and continue to learn. The journey is as important as the destination.

Finally, whatever you intend to do as a result of this book, start doing it now. The only way to learn is by doing. The sooner you start to do things differently, the more effective you will be. Remember the words of the Chinese proverb, 'The journey of a thousand miles begins with a single step'. Take that step now.

References

[1]   Kanter, R M (1981) *The Change Masters*. George Allen & Unwin, London.

For more information on the consultancy services offered in support of managing pressure, employee involvement, or other programmes related to the management of change please contact Stephen Williams at:

Resource Systems
Claro Court
Claro Road
Harrogate
England
HG1 4BA

Suggestions for further reading

1. *Living with Stress* (1991) by Cary L Cooper, Rachel D Cooper and Lynn H Eaker. Published by Penguin.

   This book is an excellent general introduction to stress and pressure. It looks at the nature of stress, stress at work, stress at home, dangerous lifestyles, learning to relax and overcoming stress. It shows why low levels of stress are positively desirable, and why today's business world and new patterns of family life make us all vulnerable. The book gives a good overview of research into stress at work and provides several self-completion questionnaires and a good discussion on coping behaviours.

2. *The Goal* (2nd ed) (1993) by Eliyahu M Goldratt and Jeff Cox. Published by Gower Publishing Company Ltd.

   The Goal is a management text book written as a novel. It tells the story of a harried plant manager who is working ever more desperately to improve his performance. The book explains how, after being given only 90 days to save his plant, he is able to break out of the conventional ways of thinking and see what needs to be done. Goldratt explains in a very readable way the ideas which underlie the theory of constraints and *The Goal* provides a different way of looking at the world. Although it has a manufacturing bias, the ideas contained in the book are relevant to anyone with managerial responsibility.

3. *Introducing Neurolinguistic Programming - the New Psychology of Personal Excellence* (1993) by Joseph O'Connor and John Seymour. Published by Mandala.

   This book is a good general introduction to Neuro Linguistic Programming (NLP). It gives a good practical introduction to improving communication skills and includes topics such as:

   • how to create rapport with others;

   • influencing skills;

   • understanding and using body language;

   • how to think about and achieve the results you want;

   • the art of asking key questions;

   • effective meetings, negotiation and selling;

   • accelerated learning strategies;

   • how to run your nervous system.

   This book is also useful because it gives an extensive bibliography, and advice on choosing books and NLP training courses. It is a good introduction but not all the sections will be relevant for everybody.

4. *Unlimited Power* (1989) by Anthony Robbins. Published by Simon & Schuster.

   This is a very readable and comprehensive book which deals with positive thinking, modelling excellence and improving communications. The book is written in a very upbeat, 'west coast' style, but contains some excellent insights into personal change.

5. *Getting to Yes* (6th ed) (1992) by Roger Fisher, William Hurey and Bruce Pattern. Published by Century Business.

   This is primarily a book on negotiating skills written by members of the Harvard Law School negotiation project. Although it is aimed at people involved in negotiating deals, it is a useful book on improving communications. It deals with issues such as separating the people from the problem using objective criteria, finding options for mutual gain and so on. The book is a valuable guide to managing the pressure caused by negotiating with your superiors, subordinates or colleagues, as well as outside suppliers or customers.

6. *The Age of Unreason* (1991) by Charles Handy. Published by Arrow.

   Charles Handy is the visiting professor at the London Business School and *The Age of Unreason* is a stimulating book which looks at the way that the world is changing and the need to respond to that change. It looks at issues such as:

   • the structure of organisations

   • new relationships between employer and employees

   • career development and the changes in society.

7. *Doing it Now* (1985) by Edwin Bliss. Published by Futura Publications.

   This is a short, easy to read book which deals with some elements of time management and is particularly good at managing procrastination.

8. *The One Minute Manager* series (1983) by Kenneth Blanchard. Published by Fontana.

   These are classic self-improvement books, and are very short and easy to read. Books in the series include:

   The One Minute Manager; Putting the One Minute Manager to Work; The One Minute Sales Manager; Leadership and the One Minute Manager; The One Minute Manager Meets the Monkey.

   Blanchard and his co-authors have some excellent ideas on managing people. The sections on goal setting, praising and delegation are particularly relevant to managing pressure.

9. *The Games People Play* (1989) by Eric Berne. Published by Penguin.

   This is the original. It provides a witty and very sensible analysis of the 'games' we play in order to live with one another – and with ourselves.

   It is an excellent if somewhat 'clinical' introduction to the field of transactional analysis.

10. *I'm OK, You're OK* (1986) by Thomas A Harris. Published by Pan Books Limited.

   This practical guide to transactional analysis is a good starting point to the subject. The book explains the developments in the field of transactional analysis in straightforward, non-technical language.

11. *The 12-Week Executive Health Plan* (1993) by Dr David Ashton. Published by Kogan Page Ltd.

   This book is described in Chapter 4 and provides an effective and practical programme for improving health and fitness.

Index

Index